Shakespeare and New Historicist Theory

Neema Parvini

Bloomsbury Arden Shakespeare
An imprint of Bloomsbury Publishing Plc
BLOOMSBURY
LONDON • OXFORD • NEW YORK • NEW DELHI • SYDNEY

Bloomsbury Arden Shakespeare
An imprint of Bloomsbury Publishing Plc

Imprint previously known as Arden Shakespeare

50 Bedford Square
London
WC1B 3DP
UK

1385 Broadway
New York
NY 10018
USA

www.bloomsbury.com

BLOOMSBURY, THE ARDEN SHAKESPEARE and the Diana logo are trademarks of Bloomsbury Publishing Plc

First published 2017

British Library Cataloguing-in-Publication Data
A catalogue record for this book is available from the British Library.

ISBN: HB: 978-1-4742-4099-4
PB: 978-1-4742-4098-7
ePDF: 978-1-4742-4102-1
ePub: 978-1-4742-4100-7

Library of Congress Cataloging-in-Publication Data
A catalog record for this book is available from the Library of Congress.

Series design by Sutchinda Thompson, cover design by Dani Leigh
Cover image © Ascophyllum nodosum (Nick Veasey / gettyimages.co.uk)

Series: Shakespeare and Theory

Typeset by Fakenham Prepress Solutions, Fakenham, Norfolk NR21 8NN
Printed and bound in Great Britain

CONTENTS

SERIES EDITOR'S PREFACE

'Asking questions about literary texts – that's literary criticism. Asking "Which questions shall we ask about literary texts?" – that's literary theory.' So goes my explanation of the current state of English studies, and Shakespeare studies, in my never-ending attempt to demystify, and simplify, theory for students in my classrooms. Another way to put it is that theory is a systematic account of the nature of literature, the act of writing, and the act of reading.

One of the primary responsibilities of any academic discipline – whether in the natural sciences, the social sciences, or the humanities – is to examine its methodologies and tools of analysis. Particularly at a time of great theoretical ferment, such as that which has characterized English studies, and Shakespeare studies, in recent years, it is incumbent upon scholars in a given discipline to provide such reflection and analysis. We all construct meanings in Shakespeare's texts and culture. Shouldering responsibility for our active role in constructing meanings in literary texts, moreover, constitutes a theoretical stance. To the extent that we examine our own critical premises and operations, that theoretical stance requires reflection on our part. It requires honesty, as well. It is thereby a fundamentally radical act. All critical analysis puts into practice a particular set of theoretical premises. Theory occurs from a particular standpoint. There is no critical practice that is somehow devoid of theory. There is no critical practice that is not implicated in theory. A common-sense, transparent encounter with any text is thereby impossible. Indeed, to the extent that theory requires us to question anew that with which we thought we were familiar, that which we thought we understood, theory constitutes a critique of common sense.

Since the advent of postmodernism, the discipline of English studies has undergone a seismic shift. And the discipline of Shakespeare studies has been at the epicentre of this shift. Indeed, it has been Shakespeare scholars who have played a major role in several of the theoretical and critical developments (e.g. new historicism, cultural materialism, presentism) that have shaped the discipline of English studies in recent years. Yet a comprehensive scholarly analysis of these crucial developments has yet to be done, and is long overdue. As the first series to foreground analysis of contemporary theoretical developments in the discipline of Shakespeare studies, *Arden Shakespeare and Theory* aims to fill a yawning gap.

To the delight of some and the chagrin of others, since 1980 or so, theory has dominated Shakespeare studies. *Arden Shakespeare and Theory* focuses on the state of the art at the outset of the twenty-first century. For the first time, it provides a comprehensive analysis of the theoretical developments that are emerging at the present moment, as well as those that are dominant or residual in Shakespeare studies.

Each volume in the series aims to offer the reader the following components: to provide a clear definition of a particular theory; to explain its key concepts; to trace its major developments, theorists, and critics; to perform a reading of a Shakespeare text; to elucidate a specific theory's intersection with or relationship to other theories; to situate it in the context of contemporary political, social, and economic developments; to analyse its significance in Shakespeare studies; and to suggest resources for further investigation. Authors of individual volumes thereby attempt to strike a balance, bringing their unique expertise, experience, and perspectives to bear upon particular theories while simultaneously fulfilling the common purpose of the series. Individual volumes in the series are devoted to elucidating particular theoretical perspectives, such as cultural materialism, ecocriticism, ecofeminism, economic theory, feminism, film theory, new historicism, postcolonialism, posthumanism, presentism, psychoanalysis, queer theory, and race theory.

Arden Shakespeare and Theory aims to enable scholars, teachers, and students alike to define their own theoretical strategies and refine their own critical practices. And students have as much at stake in these theoretical and critical enterprises – in the reading and the writing practices that characterize our discipline – as do scholars and teachers. Janus-like, the series looks forward as well as backward, serving as an inspiration and a guide for new work in Shakespeare studies at the outset of the twenty-first century, on the one hand, and providing a retrospective analysis of the intellectual labour that has been accomplished in recent years, on the other.

To return to the beginning: what is at stake in our reading of literary texts? Once we come to understand the various ways in which theory resonates with not only Shakespeare's texts, and literary texts, but the so-called 'real' world – the world outside the world of the mind, the world outside the world of academia – then we come to understand that theory is capable of powerfully enriching not only our reading of Shakespeare's texts, and literary texts, but our lives.

Evelyn Gajowski
Series Editor
University of Nevada, Las Vegas

ACKNOWLEDGEMENTS

A massive thank you to Evelyn Gajowski for making this book possible, indeed, it would not exist at all without her: a very supportive editor; Hugh Grady for his extremely generous comments and suggestions; Marion Wynne-Davies for being such a fantastic colleague and for her valuable suggestions; Adeline Johns-Putra for being an equally fantastic colleague and for helping me understand the ways in which 'new historicism' as practised by scholars of the Romantic period differs from its early modern variant; Margaret Bartley and Emily Hockley from Bloomsbury, a pleasure to work with them on another book; Stephen Greenblatt for his graciousness and magnanimity in our communications, and for providing greater clarity on his relationship with Marxism. Much gratitude also to my parents for their love and support, and especially to my mother for not only watching *Measure for Measure* with me and giving me much to think about but also for reading the whole manuscript. And finally to Sarah Frazer for her love, understanding and help.

INTRODUCTORY NOTE

New historicism has at this point been endlessly summarized in critical anthologies, student guides and in various attacks and critiques, to the point where it is reduced almost to a handful of oft-repeated slogans. In many of these summaries, it has to share space with cultural materialism, a school that has a completely different theoretical genesis and set of aims, despite its emerging at the same time and sometimes even publishing in the same volumes. New historicism has always been diffuse and its practitioners have sought to resist easy categorization. But this has not stopped the aforementioned summaries constructing their own version of what new historicism stands for. As these accounts pile up, they become their own edifice. The author of one critical companion goes to another such companion, and checks it against an introduction to literary theory, or two, and so on – and the unspoken fact is that those authors are all doing the same thing. Fairly soon, a conventional narrative around new historicism builds up. After this narrative has been repeated often enough, it is this version of new historicism that scholars come to know. New historicism has been for lack of a better term 'text-bookised'.

Between these pages, I have a rare and perhaps even unique opportunity to conduct a book-length scholarly investigation into new historicism as it pertains to the study of Shakespeare's literary work. And I am grateful to be afforded the space to go well beyond such standard accounts. It is my aim to problematize, if not completely dismantle, the aforementioned narrative. This is not to say that the 'new historicism' defined by such accounts is a total fiction, but rather to recognize that it has been written in crude shorthand.

Chapter 1 provides a detailed introduction and initial interrogation of new historicism. It focuses on historiography, and attempts to gain a sense of a new historicist 'theory of history' by reading Catherine Gallagher and Stephen Greenblatt's *Practising New Historicism* (2000) alongside some of their progenitors such as Michel Foucault, Hayden White and Clifford Geertz. It also spends some time pitting against each other two great historians of the early modern period, G. R. Elton and Fernand Braudel, in a bid to see more clearly where new historicism fits into the historiographical landscape of broader twentieth-century trends. Chapter 2 concerns itself with literary history that was produced in Shakespeare studies after E. M. W. Tillyard, but before Stephen Greenblatt, to gain a greater understanding of how new historicism distinguished itself from its immediate predecessors. This chapter focuses mainly on works by Francis Fergusson, C. L. Barber, Wilbur Sanders and Stephen Orgel. Chapter 3 looks directly at a range of new historicist studies by practitioners such as Stephen Greenblatt, Louis Montrose, Jonathan Goldberg and Leonard Tennenhouse, and asks a key question: where is the 'counterhistory' that Gallagher and Greenblatt spoke so much about in *Practising New Historicism*? It also focuses on the attempt to re-label new historicism as 'cultural poetics'. Chapter 4 is a case study in which I trace the impact and consequences of new historicism on a single play, *Measure for Measure*, looking at readings by Goldberg, Tennenhouse, Greenblatt, Steven Mullaney, Leah S. Marcus and Craig A. Bernthall. Chapter 5 focuses on the intersection between new historicism and feminism, and what has, at times, been a fraught relationship. Chapter 6 contemplates afresh some of the salient criticisms put forth by opponents of new historicism in the light of the preceding five chapters. Finally, Chapter 7 considers historicist practice after new historicism and its interest in the 'everyday', and offers a brief conclusion that considers the legacy of new historicism.

1

What is 'History'?

It seems appropriate to start a book about new historicism with an anecdote. I once gave a lecture at the British Museum to members of the general public. I was trying to give them a sense of why the idea of Shakespeare as universal genius is no longer accepted by many in the academy. My basic plan was to tell this story only to turn stunningly back on it to reveal that I do, in fact, believe Shakespeare possessed a genius that, while not 'universal' exactly, gave him unique insights into the human condition that might be classed as broadly transhistorical. It was to be a great crowd-pleasing crescendo to the talk. For this to work, however, it was necessary to detour briefly and explain a couple of the basic theoretical tenets that have been so influential in dismantling the received wisdom accepting Shakespeare's universality. I had a projection slide or two on Louis Althusser, and maybe another on Michel Foucault. During this theoretical portion of the lecture, one gentlemen in the audience stood up and shouted, 'I thought this was meant to be about Shakespeare!' He huffed and puffed, and then he walked out. I concluded the lecture, complete with the planned crescendo, and, aside from the disgruntled heckler, it seemed to go down very well with my audience. But, obviously, the moment has stayed with me. Why did that man walk out? And why was it so difficult to explain to a lay audience, from outside the academy, the impact of new historicist thinking on our view of Shakespeare?

In the prospect of writing this study, I am faced with a rather different proposition. Many of my readers (i.e. those 'inside the academy') will already know, however roughly, the 'story' of how the death of 'the universal bard' came to pass. My aim is to complicate and flesh out that story to the point where we can come to a new or at least modified understanding of exactly what has taken place in the past thirty or forty years of Shakespeare scholarship and criticism. But still I am reminded of the man's cry – 'I thought this was meant to be about Shakespeare!' – as I write. I say this now because I'm afraid that there will be large sections of this book that are not directly 'about Shakespeare'. In fact, my first three chapters are much more about historiography, literary theory and the critical process. And we will not encounter Shakespeare directly until the case study on *Measure for Measure* in Chapter 4. He is in the background: a reference point, an implied yet deferred object of ultimate study, rather than the centre of focus. This is not so much a warning as it is an indication that a true account of new historicism cannot come about solely by looking at Shakespeare's plays or sonnets. The approach did not evolve immanently from a direct engagement with Shakespeare, but, rather, brought a whole range of influences from other disciplines to bear on the study of early modern literature (of which Shakespeare is the most visible constituent). I must turn from Shakespeare, then, and will instead begin with a question …

What is history? There seems an obvious answer: it is the past. But will that suffice? 'History' certainly consists of 'the past', but does it contain all of the past? 'The past' is clearly 'in history', but is it actually 'history' in and of itself? In very simple terms, we might inch towards a definition by saying that 'the past' is 'what happened', in real-time, whereas 'history' is a record of the past constructed by human beings. 'The past' is indiscriminate and stretches infinitely. It is also unrecoverable; to all intents and purposes it is 'lost' for all time. Think of Jean-Paul Sartre's banana that must be 'eaten on the spot' it falls lest it lose the freshness of its taste;[1] the past is the lost moment of freshness that is never to return. Anything that occurred before the 'here and now' constitutes 'the past'. 'History', on the other hand, even though it *refers* to this lost past, exists in the 'here and now'. 'History' does not exist independently of people. Not only must it be recorded and written, it must also be told and remembered. In effect, history exists only when it is read or acknowledged. It is also discriminatory inasmuch as it constitutes what a community chooses to remember. It has a shape and scope crafted by people. It tells a story. It is not simply a record of the past, it has heroes and villains, winners and losers and great events that produce seismic ripple effects. Of course, no one knew this better than Shakespeare, who used history as the raw material of so many of his plays. Let me ask another question then: if 'history' is intrinsically such a man-made construct, does it follow, therefore, that there must be a 'theory of history'? Even the most passing and rudimentary knowledge of historiography reveals that, implicitly or explicitly, and whether or not historians will admit it, there are guiding principles that the writers of 'history' follow, which have changed over time.

I am writing this book at an interesting juncture for Shakespeare studies, and the story of why it is interesting is told partly in its title *Shakespeare and New Historicist Theory*. Some readers may indeed think of the title as being oxymoronic, especially at the sight of the two words 'Historicist' and 'Theory' being set side-by-side. In 2012, one distinguished Professor of English – whom some might class as a new historicist, and whose work is certainly very strongly historicist in its approach – told me that theory is 'now virtually dead in the US though apparently on life support in the UK'.[2] To a certain mode of thinking 'historicism' and 'theory' are antithetical. Even as far back as 1986 Jean E. Howard expressed concerns. 'There is a real danger that the emerging interest in history will be appropriated by those wishing to suppress or erase the theoretical revolution that has gone on in the last several decades. Ironically, the "new history" may well turn out to be a backlash phenomenon:

a flight from theory'.[3] 'New Historicism' does not so much represent a coherent 'theory' as one might find written by a philosopher or literary theorist, but rather a general approach to literature underpinned by a loose set of common aims and practices. As Fredric Jameson put it, new historicism has long maintained 'a highly theoretical reluctance to "theorize"'.[4] It is notable that in their attempt to sum up their work, in 2000, Stephen Greenblatt and Catherine Gallagher called their book *Practising New Historicism*, rather than *Theorising New Historicism*. In fact, as they put it themselves, they 'became rather good at slipping out of theoretical nooses'. They advocate what they call a 'total immersion in practice', and freely admit that new historicism is 'insufficiently theorized' – but they seem to like it that way.[5] Since 2000, and perhaps long before, the general trend has been to favour praxis over theory. Indeed, there was a slew of publications at the turn of the millennium officially signalling that we are now working in a 'post-theory' moment,[6] and many within the discipline seem to have taken the 'after theory' idea literally to mean that it is simply something we don't 'do' anymore. Douglas Bruster declared in 2003 that new historicism was officially dead, killed by its own assimilation.[7] Yet over a decade later, historicism is still by far the most dominant strain among critical approaches to Shakespeare, to the point where it can appear an almost unshakable orthodoxy. However, the bulk of work produced in the past fifteen years has had a certain antiquarian temper – more 'straight-forwardly historical' than the seminal and virtuoso new historicist studies of the 1980s. It seems to me that to a large extent new historicism has given way to plain old literary history, David Scott Kastan's 'New Boredom'.[8] And often that literary history is openly hostile to 'theory' and sets itself up almost in opposition to it. So why 'New Historicist Theory' in the title? Consider again what I've just outlined: history and theory are not opposites and any historical practice in some sense presupposes a 'theory of history'. I hope to show, among other things, that the hostility towards theory shown by certain practitioners of literary history is not only misplaced but also profoundly ironic considering new historicism's intellectual roots.

Throughout this book I am going to keep two questions in focus. First, what is the 'theory of history' advocated by new historicism, whether explicitly or implicitly? And second, what kinds of work can we consider 'properly new historicist'? 'New historicism' has become quite a nebulous term, and has been notoriously difficult to pin down. Furthermore, its practitioners have always been curiously reluctant to embrace the label and, as one commentator wryly put it, 'exceptionally unwilling to stand together for a team photograph'.[9] My aim in keeping these questions in focus is a bid to get to the heart of what it is (or was) really about. In so doing, I hope to assess new historicism's contribution to Shakespeare studies. In the interests of full disclosure, I should mention that your author is not a new historicist himself, and he has been strongly critical of the approach in print before now.[10] This book does not aim to replicate those critiques, and instead takes the form of a scholarly enquiry into new historicism in a bid to gain a holistic understanding of its genesis (Chapters 1 and 2), its major practitioners (Chapters 3 and 4), its complex relationship with feminism (Chapter 5), opponents (Chapter 6), successors and legacy (Chapter 7). One of my key objectives is to make this book more comprehensive and nuanced than previous accounts of new historicism, and, as stated, to complicate and sometimes challenge the standard narratives that have sprung up around it.

New historicism, since its advent in 1980, has arguably been more influential to Shakespeare studies than any other approach, at least within the academy. Certain figures loom large in the history of Shakespeare criticism and scholarship: Edward Dowden, A. C. Bradley, L. C. Knights, E. M. W. Tillyard, John Dover Wilson, W. W. Greg, William Empson, F. R. Leavis, A. P. Rossiter, G. K Hunter, Jan Kott, among many others. But none of them had a greater impact than Stephen Greenblatt in terms of transforming the very *modus operandi* of what a Shakespeare critic 'does'. One might make a case that A. C. Bradley's Shakespeare is the one that has most filtered through to the popular imagination (often through the hidden filter of the school classroom) – indeed, the shorthand view of *Hamlet*, for example, being a play about why its protagonist procrastinates surely has its genesis in Bradley (as the culmination of nineteenth-century thinking on the play, in the tradition of Goethe and Coleridge), and we might say the same about popular views of any of the tragic heroes. One might make a case that Jan Kott has been the most influential critic in terms of Shakespeare on stage: the production history of *King Lear* has certainly felt the impact of *Shakespeare Our Contemporary*. But within the academy itself – in terms of what sort of work Shakespeareans have produced, and in terms of what undergraduates study at university – Greenblatt and new historicism have been far-reaching, and in the space of less than a decade, the 1980s, have overturned and utterly transformed the status quo to become the new orthodoxy, especially in the United States.

In the years before new historicism, from the 1940s to the 1970s, across the discipline, the formalism of the New Criticism dominated the study of English literature. However, in the domain of Shakespeare studies, perhaps owing to the fact that Shakespeare himself is so closely identified with the late Elizabethan era and with the London of that period, historicist scholarship never quite gave way to a purely textual analysis of the plays (more on this in Chapter 2). This is to say that it would be incorrect to characterize new historicism as 'rescuing' Shakespeare studies from the grip of a staid formalism through the introduction of context and history. Context and history were *always* there, and the label of being 'new' historicism tacitly acknowledges that. It is important to make this clear because many accounts paint a different picture: as if new historicism's chief achievement were to bring history to literature after decades of hermetically sealed textual work. This is simply not true. 'History' had always been done in Shakespeare scholarship and criticism. The key departure made by Stephen Greenblatt and others was in bringing historical approaches and ways of thinking about history from other disciplines (history, anthropology, philosophy) to bear on the study of Shakespeare and his contemporaries.

In the remainder of this chapter, I am going to come to a sense of what new historicism's 'theory of history' might be, primarily by way of reading *Practising New Historicism* (2000) against a backdrop of three key theoretical influences: Michel Foucault, the philosopher, whose work on power and discourse seemed a virtual obsession to practitioners of new historicism in the 1980s and early 1990s; Hayden White, the historian, most famous for his book *Metahistory* (1973); Clifford Geertz, the anthropologist, whose enormously influential collection of essays, *The Interpretation of Cultures* (1973), arguably provided the blueprint for much of Stephen Greenblatt's approach to literature. Before that, however, I wish to take a sustained look at an often overlooked influence: the 'theory of history' put forward by Fernand Braudel, often associated with the *Annales School*, whose masterpiece *The Mediterranean and the Mediterranean World in the Age of Philip II* (1949) is directly relevant to our period and whose mammoth three-volume *Civilization and Capitalism, 15th–18th Centuries* (1981) represents a huge achievement in historical research.

This is not to say that these four thinkers were the only ones to influence new historicism, of course: Marxist theorists such as Antonio Gramsci and Foucault's old mentor, Louis Althusser, played a formative (if, in the end, thoroughly disavowed) part;[11] Greenblatt studied under Raymond Williams at Cambridge and devotes much space to him in *Practising New Historicism*, and other new historicists often seem taken with his dynamic view of shifting cultures. Williams is preferred, at any rate, to that other British Marxist stalwart of literary theory, Terry Eagleton, who, as Harold Veeser once said, new historicists 'consider ... an old fart'.[12] Arguments might be made for Dominick Lacapra being more crucial to the view of history as narrative than Hayden White (although I'd argue he came too late);[13] and it was Fredric Jameson who famously said 'always historicize'.[14] But for our purposes, as regards theories of history, Foucault, White and Geertz are the three most important progenitors, with Braudel a crucial figure in the academic background of the period, whose work, even by way of contrast, can show us the real nature of new historicist work. This may appear counter-intuitive to some: Williams, for example, was much more direct and obvious an influence on Greenblatt than Braudel ever was (he is not even mentioned in *Practising New Historicism*, although he is acknowledged as the inspiration behind the edited collection *New World Encounters*, and he is cited, if only briefly, in *Renaissance Self-Fashioning*[15]). But it seems to me that the notion of 'counter-history', which is apparently so central to new historicism, owes more to Braudel and the Annalistes than it does to the much more theoretical and abstract work of Williams (who was most influential on the cultural materialists);[16] and Braudel's influence on Foucault has perhaps been underplayed. Indeed, all four of these theorists of history and culture might be grouped loosely, as being against the grain of mainstream history as carried out by conventional historians, and, with the possible exception of Geertz (who was opposed to Claude Lévi-Strauss), they were all structuralists. By the end of the chapter, my reasons for highlighting these thinkers in particular (at the expense of other influences) should become more obvious.

However, before getting to them, it is paramount to gain a sense of the type of history that all these thinkers were in some sense reacting to, writing against, and ultimately aiming to replace – not least because clarity can often come from contrast. It is fair to say that mainstream historians in the Anglo-sphere were always sceptical of 'theories of history'. And in that scepticism we can detect that, 'characteristic', form of stubbornly down-to-earth-Oxbridge practicality that refuses to believe that anything that isn't rolling up one's sleeves and getting on with the actual work of scholarly practice can possibly be of any value. We can nowhere better recognize that than in the writings of an old-fashioned historian of the Tudor period such as G. R. Elton, who was a major figure in the Cambridge History department for many years. The young Greenblatt would have known him, at least through reputation, not least because he was arguably the world's most eminent expert on the reign of Henry VIII, and in particular on the figures of Thomas Cromwell and Thomas More (in whose *Utopia* Greenblatt has always maintained a special interest).[17] Let us get a real measure of what Elton's 'theory of history' might have been (although if he were sitting here I'd imagine he might scowl at the idea of my attributing him with any *theory* of history at all). In 1967, Elton wrote a manifesto of his approach called *The Practice of History*, incidentally written in response to E. H. Carr's *What is History?* (1961), from which this chapter borrows its title. By Elton's own admission, his book

> embodies an assumption that the study and writing of history are justified in themselves, and reflects a suspicion that a philosophic concern with such problems as the reality of historical knowledge or the nature of historical thought only hinders the practice of history. When I read discussions of how historians think, how they can claim to describe what no longer exists, or whether historical fact has an existence independent of the thinker about facts, I marvel at the ingenuity of the writers, for usually they are men who have never apparently themselves tried to do the work, to see the manifestly surviving of past fact and event, or to practice critical judgement on the materials of history, rather than the minds of historians.[18]

Elton is palpably angered by what he sees as little more than armchair commentators who can't possibly understand what the study of history really entails because they are not historians themselves. In the footnotes, he adds, caustically: 'Every new number of *History and Theory* is liable to contain yet another article struggling to give history a philosophic base, and some of them are interesting. But they do not, I fear, advance the writing of history.'[19] In 1990, approaching his seventieth birthday and four years before his death, Elton – by this point a dinosaur – was still banging the drum against theory or philosophy or any other discipline interfering with his beloved 'History'. He was aware that he was

> defending what may appear to be very old-fashioned convictions and practices [...] [I]t does not matter which [...] [interpretative and ideological] theory we choose: they all arise from the same ambition and do equal harm to the independent understanding of the past [...] most theory-mongers like to make our flesh creep.[20]

A vitriolic Elton goes as far as to speak of the 'theory-frozen mind'. He decries most of all the trend of different theoretical models coming in and out of fashion: 'yesterday's buzz-words are today's incomprehensible obscurities'. He criticises the *Annales* school for leaving too 'much uncontrolled speculation in the hands of the historian', and in the next line dismisses Clifford Geertz on whom he has almost nothing to say beyond the fact that he is revered in the United States.

> Thus fashions come and go. We have had history written to the model of society as a depository of universal myth (a la Lévi-Strauss) or of coded messages saying that all forms of knowledge are only forms of power (Foucault) [...] None of these theories wished to undermine the writing of history; they thought they were giving it shape and substance. Two things were common to them all: they made possible the construction of impossible-looking edifices, and they told us much more about the present within which their promoters worked than about the past.[21]

He even has some ire for literary theory, which he finds 'comprehensively menacing' and 'particularly insidious in the United States where the intellectual community (as it styles itself) is always inclined to accept most humbly the latest fashions'. But he reserves a special contempt for the French post-structuralists, decrying their postmodern theories as 'the intellectual equivalent of crack', and the 'cancerous radiation that comes from the foreheads of [Jacques] Derrida and Foucault'.[22]

It would be easy to characterize Elton by this point in his career as the archetypal grouchy old man telling the kids to get off the lawn of 'History', but it is clear from his ranting that he feels that recent theoretical approaches to history have destroyed methods that he thinks are essential for producing good and accurate history. What are they? In short, following the tradition of Leopold von Ranke, a meticulous examination of primary sources guided by (but at the same time controlling) a disciplined imagination free of present-day concerns (which might introduce the taint of anachronism) and free from pre-set agendas – that is, history should be studied for its own sake. He does not like the idea of 'learning from history' and warns against the temptation of seeing it as being 'relevant to the present'.[23] He wants the historian to immerse himself totally in the facts and materials of his period:

> The hallmark of the amateur is a failure of instinctive understanding. This expresses itself most clearly in the readiness to see the exceptional in the commonplace and to find the unusual ordinary. The amateur tends to find the past, or parts of it, quaint; the professional is totally incapable of this. On the other hand, the professional, truly understanding an age from the inside – living with its attitudes and prejudices – can also judge it; refusal to judge is quite as amateurish a characteristic as willingness to judge by the wrong, because anachronistic, standards.[24]

In effect, Elton's perfect historian is the expert who knows so much about the given period that even his best guesses carry some weight of accuracy.

There are two more features of Elton's approach that I must highlight to contextualize the theories that are to follow.

The first can be put very simply as a preference for the idea that the events of history are for the most part caused by the decisions of individuals – Great Men like his constitutional hero Thomas Cromwell[25] – rather than socio-economic or impersonal structural reasons; in this respect he was staunchly opposed to the Marxist view of history. The second, and perhaps even more important feature is a conviction that history is, above all, about events:

> History deals in events, not states; it investigates things that happen and not things that are. As against this, archaeology, for instance, can only uncover and describe states, conditions and circumstances particular to a way of life; it is unable to handle the fact of life, which is movement [...] Anthropology or sociology, on the other hand, may well display interest in the event – in a circumcision ceremony or a wedding, in the building of a school or the formation of an opinion – but this will not be for the sake of the event, but for the sake of extracting static conclusions from moving elements [...] History treats fundamentally of the transformation of things (people, institutions, ideas, and so on) from one state to another, and the event is its concern as well as its instrument.[26]

The full relevance of this quotation will become clear shortly. But for now, it is enough for us to know that among historians this practically-minded-back-to-basics 'evidence-first' or 'empirical' approach is known as 'analytical history' and it still has adherents today, both within and outside the academy. For example, David Starkey, who is arguably the most famous popular historian of the Tudor era in Britain today, partly owing to his frequent television appearances, was supervised by Elton when reading for his doctoral thesis – and his work bears many of the hallmarks of his old mentor. This is to say that, although Elton rather crankily presented himself as being old-fashioned, his idea of, and approach to, history remains embedded in the mainstream imagination.

It is important to remember too, that Elton saw himself as speaking up for working historians who did not have a voice in these meta-historical debates; that is not to say that they all agree with him, but it would be fair to say that, especially in Britain and America, suspicion of postmodern ideas among certain historians remains deep and very real. His concerns that the tools of history might be under threat were echoed even by some of his most bitter academic enemies, such as Lawrence Stone.[27]

Let us turn now to Fernand Braudel, whose influence on new historicism is indirect, diffuse, and very seldom, if ever, acknowledged. In over two dozen available accounts of new historicism (which I will not list here, though I did check) – including my own – Braudel is not cited even once. There are four possible reasons for this. First, these accounts are almost entirely written by academics from within the discipline of English literature who, despite 'working historically', typically do not engage the discipline of History or its internal historiographical debates head on. Second, space – which I am grateful to be afforded here – will not allow for much more than an obligatory summary of the influence of Foucault and Geertz (who have become in some respects reduced to the same few oft-repeated slogans), sometimes Williams (misplaced in my view), and, much more rarely, White. Third, it must be understood that Braudel's influence over twentieth-century history (as a discipline) is what Bob Dylan's might be to twentieth-century music, that is: incalculable. He is a towering figure, seen by many (especially in France) as the most important historian since the end of the Second World War, whose influence may touch work even where it is not immediately obvious. And fourth – and this is, I think, the most valid reason – his emphasis on the materiality of history is at odds with new historicism's insistence on a textual history. As I hope to show, a fuller understanding of what Braudel's vision of history entails will help us see much more clearly the theoretical moves made by new historicism and its progenitors. Later in this book (see especially Chapter 7), it will also help us understand some of the developments that took place in Shakespeare studies after new historicism.

Braudel's 'theory of history' makes for a sharp contrast to that espoused by Elton. Unlike Elton, Braudel does not see history as being mainly about the deeds of great individuals, and neither does he think that 'the event' is its key. For Braudel, a view such as Elton's is short-termist and does not give a true reflection of a particular place at a particular time. Or, rather, it is only focusing on 'one layer' of that time, what he calls *histoire événementielle* (the history of events) or *courte durée* (individual time). This layer is essentially just on the surface, only skin deep:

> Everyday life consists of the little things one hardly notices in time and space. The more we reduce the focus of vision, the more likely we are to find ourselves in the environment of material life: the broad sweep usually corresponds to History with a capital letter, to distant trade routes, and the networks of national or urban economies. If we reduce the length of the time observed, we either have the event or the everyday happening. The event is, or is taken to be, unique; the everyday happening is repeated, and the more often it is repeated the more likely it is to become a generality or rather a structure. It pervades society at all levels, and characterises ways of being and behaving which are perpetuated through endless ages.[28]

Braudel states clearly his belief that the way of gaining the true measure of a given culture in any period is to uncover the 'deep structures' that govern everyday life. For him, conventional history has been much too taken up with exceptional events and therefore too quick to overestimate the importance of such events and the real rate of change: the history 'of man in his relationship to the environment' is 'a history in which all change is slow'.[29]

Beneath *courte durée* (individual time) are deeper structural layers. Immediately under it, we find social time, which comprises the social, economic and cultural (including religion). This includes the entire system of exchanges that underpins the global economy, as well as any activities that ostensibly fall outside that, such as bartering. Braudel, it must be said, seems to focus exclusively on the economic at the expense of the social and cultural (or indeed religious). At times, his work reads like a more fully-fleshed and densely researched version of *Capital* by Karl Marx, but this is partly owing to the fact that he intended his work to be read alongside that of his colleague, Lucien Febvre, who founded the *Annales* school with Marc Bloch.[30] The third and deepest layer is geographical time (*la longue durée*), which comprises the whole way of material life: the total population, the total availability of land, the type of land, the types of crops available, the types of animals native to a region, food, the weather, the environment, the shape of the coastline and so on. Geographical time concerns the relationship of the people to their (physical) environment – or, as he describes it in the quotation above, 'the everyday life'.

Both of Braudel's two most famous works, *The Mediterranean and the Mediterranean World in the Age of Philip II* and *Civilization and Capitalism, 15th–18th Centuries*, are structured according to these three categorizations of time (the former in three parts over two volumes, and the latter in three volumes, although there is no section dedicated to *courte durée*). In each case, the first volume deals in exhaustive and minute, at times awe-inspiring, detail with the *longue durée*: the entire material life of the period in question. This is perhaps the type of work for which Braudel is most famous and it is typically dubbed 'geo-history'. In Part 1 of *The Mediterranean* he restricts this very largely to the areas around the Mediterranean, and confines his focus to the 1500s. In the first volume of *Civilization and Capitalism*, *The Structures of Everyday Life*, he somehow manages to do this for the entire world, covering every continent and the period 1400–1800. These studies of the *longue durée* are extremely rich in content, detailing as they do every aspect of 'everyday life', from the different types of cereal grains consumed by peasants in different regions to the total population of those regions, reasons for their populations' rising and falling at different times, and things like when exactly items such as chairs, tables, forks and so on became commonplace. The 'panoramic' view of history is in itself fascinating, but it is curiously devoid of individual names and faces and sometimes eerily absent of events. The history that Braudel gives us in his *longue durée* is somehow full of the stuff of life – wheat, rice, corn, meat, spices of all kinds, farming, building, mending, sewing and other such 'busy work' – while being simultaneously grim, static, death-ridden, poverty-stricken and confirming the futility of endlessly looping Waiting-for-Godot-like cycles of feasting and famine. The overall effect serves to bring home the crushing reality that for the vast majority of the earth's population, essentially, 'hardly anything changed at all'.[31] For all the talk of the Renaissance, or the Ages of Discovery, Reason or the Enlightenment, most people were still peasants engaged in farm work or similar and subsisting on basic cereal crops supported by vegetables and meat. To mainstream history, of the sort written by G. R. Elton, these peasants and their everyday practices are almost entirely out of focus. They recede so far into the background that history barely acknowledges them, except when they muster together into 'events' such as revolts or rebellions. For Braudel, a true understanding of history can come only after a comprehensive and as complete as possible account of the *longue durée* has been carried out, because it is the only measure of historical change. The changes and squabbles of the elite political classes that comprise most history are merely effervescent, tiny blips on the radar, if the whole way of life in real, material terms has not been touched.

Braudel's practice is often called 'total history', because he does not stop there. In Part 2 of *The Mediterranean*, and in *The Wheels of Commerce* (the second volume of *Civilization and Capitalism*), with the same breath-taking panoramic scope and level of detail, he maps out the vast range of human activities, systems and exchanges that consist in the economy, as well as considering other broad-level structures such as empires. The focus of this work bears at least a superficial similarity to the focus on transactions and exchanges between distinct social practices found in new historicist studies, especially those carried out by proponents of 'cultural poetics' (see Chapter 3). Then, in Part 3 of *The Mediterranean*, 'Events, Politics and People', he carries out more conventional history of the variety of which Elton might approve, but one senses that this is not where Braudel's heart lies. As one reviewer put it, 'he is never enthralled by the personal name, the battle, the date, the king, general, or admiral'[32] – it is almost as if the lens of his camera has zoomed in too close and he is struggling to widen it out again. Therefore, it is unsurprising to find that volume 3 of *Civilization and Capitalism (The Perspective of the World)* eschews this more traditional history section, with its personal names, to focus more broadly on the emergence of national markets and their role in world economies. In practice then, Braudel's real focus is squarely on the *longue durée* and on the economic aspects of 'social time'. He aims to give a history of the people as they really lived, and not of their self-appointed leaders.

There are two other crucial respects in which Braudel differs from an historian such as Elton. First, whereas Elton fiercely defends the disciplinary ramparts of history from the supposed taint of outside methods, Braudel's approach is interdisciplinary and borrows liberally from geography and economics in particular. Indeed, he seems to wish for history to be the vessel for uniting the social sciences. Second, Braudel is often willing, as a matter of necessity, to extrapolate conclusions about the everyday life of the past from limited and even anecdotal evidence:

> Sometimes a few anecdotes are enough to set up a signal which points to a way of life. There is a drawing which shows Maximilian of Austria at table, in about 1513: he is

putting his hand into a dish. Two centuries or so later, the Princess Palatine tells how Louis XIV, when he allowed his children to sit up to table for the first time, forbade them to eat differently from him, and in particular to eat with a fork as an over-zealous tutor had taught them. So when did Europe invent table manners?[33]

In fact, the account of the development of table manners, found later in *The Structures of Everyday Life*,[34] reads almost as if Braudel were a detective (perhaps more Jules Maigret than Inspector Clouseau) finding clues in medieval and Renaissance paintings and sifting them for evidence of forks, plates, silverware and so on. But perhaps Braudel's point is that no other historian before him (or at least not before the *Annales* school) would have thought the history of the fork might be worthy of such investigation. And Braudel's entire corpus is much like this: one chapter after the other of these little investigations uncovering the fragments of the past piece-by-piece, to put together the massive jigsaw of what 'everyday life' must have looked like. And he is well aware that this is his method:

Material life, of course, presents itself to us in the anecdotal form of thousands and thousands of assorted facts. Can we call these events? No: to do so would be to inflate their importance, to grant them a significance they never had. That the Holy Roman Emperor Maximilian ate with his fingers from the dishes at a banquet (as we can see from a drawing) is an everyday detail, not an event. So is the story about the bandit Cartouche, on the point of execution, preferring a glass of wine to the coffee he was offered. This is the dust of history, microhistory in the same sense that Georges Gurvitch talks about micro-sociology: little facts which do, it is true, by indefinite repetition, add up to form linked chains. Each of them represents the thousands of others that have crossed the silent depths of time and *endured*.[35]

We can see something of this approach to history in new historicism. There is the same commitment in Braudel's counter-historical work to 'break the continuities of *grand réctis*, to hear the voices of history's excluded' that new historicists found so attractive in Foucault.[36]

In *Practising New Historicism*, Gallagher and Greenblatt talk about their use of anecdotes in reference almost exclusively to Williams and Foucault, but surely here, in Braudel, is where we can find 'the touch of the real' on which they are so keen.[37] In fact, paradoxically, this is where we might detect the greatest difference between Braudel and the new historicists, and the limits of his indirect influence. It is also an opportune moment to start to change our focus from Braudel towards Foucault. It is clear that Foucault's methods were influenced by Braudel and the others from the *Annales* school; and Braudel himself even dubbed Foucault's *Madness and Civilization* '*prison de longue durée*'.[38] As Colin Koopman writes, 'Braudel's influence on historical thought was felt everywhere, and deeply so, in the decades in which Foucault was writing [...] A fuller understanding of Braudel would probably inform our understanding of Foucault'.[39] Braudel's conception of history was essentially a form of historical materialism, and he was committed to finding causes for phenomena. Although change in the *longue durée* is glacial, for Braudel, there is still a causal relationship between the past and present and a dialogical relationship between his three types of time. While Braudel always insists on the importance of social time, it is fair to say that his emphasis is in the vast majority of cases on economic or material causes. Finally, his wide-lens view of history – which de-emphasizes the role of leaders such as Philip II of Spain, who he says 'were, despite their illusions, more acted upon than actors'[40] – is, in the end deterministic and practically obliterates the scope for individual agency. Note the following passage:

> I would conclude with the paradox that the true man of action is he who can measure most nearly the constraints

> upon him, who chooses to remain within them and even to take advantage of the weight of the inevitable, exerting his own pressure in the same direction. All efforts against the prevailing tide of history – which is not always obvious – are doomed to failure. So when I think of the individual, I am always inclined to see him imprisoned within a destiny in which he himself has little hand, fixed in a landscape in which the infinite perspectives of the long term stretch into the distance both behind him and before. In historical analysis as I see it, rightly or wrongly, the long run always wins in the end. Annihilating innumerable events – all those which cannot be accommodated in the main ongoing current and which are therefore ruthlessly swept to one side – it indubitably limits both the freedom of the individual and even the role of chance.[41]

This conclusion virtually crushes the individual beneath the inevitable march of *long history*. He would probably say, however, that he was being realistic rather than pessimistic. Although the means and emphasis are different, there is a certain similarity here to Foucault's idea that 'man is an invention of recent date [...] perhaps nearing its end [...] [which, if certain arrangements change] one can certainly wager that man would be erased, like a face drawn in the sand at the edge of the sea'.[42]

How does Foucault's concept of history compare? In my estimation, it is difficult to sum up a single theory of history from Foucault's works. It is more useful to think in terms of his early and late periods, broadly falling in the 1960s and 1970s respectively. The early Foucault can be classed as the author of *Madness and Civilization* (1961), *The Birth of the Clinic* (1963), The *Order of Things* (1966). The late Foucault comprises *Discipline and Punish* (1975) and the three volumes of *The History of Sexuality* (1976–84), as well as the edited collection of interviews and articles from the mid-1970s, *Power / Knowledge* (1980). *The Archaeology of Knowledge* (1969) is the bridging or transitional text between the two periods. Early

Foucault might be dubbed as the 'archaeological Foucault', whereas one might call late Foucault 'the arbiter of power'. This is not to say that there is a 'rupture' in his thought, but rather that the intense focus on discourse and power found in the later Foucault is really only implied in the earlier work.

Early Foucault makes a similar distinction to that of Braudel in distinguishing between a surface-level history of the ideas of individuals (*connaissance*, i.e. particular types of knowledge, 'biology or economics for example') and the analysis of deeper and more fundamental structures (*savoir*).

> Like Braudel, Foucault rejects [traditional history] [...] which assumes that the phenomena it deals with are unified around a single center (the progress of mankind, final scientific truth) in favor of "general history". The latter allows that its phenomena may form disparate series that cannot be reduced to a unity, but without insisting that these series are entirely independent. General intellectual history seeks to describe the complex interrelations of mutually irreducible discursive formations.[43]

The crucial difference, however, is that where Braudel's *longue durée* refers to the material way of life, Foucault's *savoir* refers exclusively to the realm of thought – it is an *intellectual* history as opposed to a material one. In fact, *savoir* 'refers to the conditions that are necessary in a particular period for this or that type of object to be given to *connaissance* and for this or that enunciation to be formulated'.[44] In short, then, if *connaissance* conditions what *is* thought, *savoir* conditions the very possibilities of what *can* be thought. Foucault sees his task as that of an 'archaeologist' digging up the rules that govern *savoir*, and for any given period he calls these rules *epistemes*.[45] Foucault's notion of history – in real contrast to both Elton's and Braudel's – is fundamentally discontinuous. He rejects entirely the narrative of continued and inevitable progress towards our modern present that 'history' since the Enlightenment has imposed on the past.

Foucault defines three broad epistemes in Western thought: the episteme before the seventeenth century had at its centre the belief that all things were connected through God, in a nutshell the belief in the 'great chain of being' outlined in E. M. W. Tillyard's *The Elizabethan World Picture*.[46] During the Renaissance, this system of thought was overthrown or 'ruptured' by the return to a classical belief in representation, which is Foucault's second episteme. It is fundamentally a belief in the power of language to represent reality, and in the almost unlimited potential of individuals who can harness that power (we might think of Prospero and his magic). And this, in turn, was ruptured in the nineteenth century by the belief that individuals are in fact limited, and accordingly their representational potential is finite because they are bound by their social context. 'Thus', says Foucault, 'European culture is inventing for itself a depth in which what matters is no longer identities, distinctive characters, permanent tables with all their possible paths and routes, but great hidden forces developed on the basis of their primitive and inaccessible nucleus, origin, causality, and history'. We might think of the more deterministic thinkers of the period, such as Karl Marx or Charles Darwin. But, for Foucault, Marx, for instance, was not the cause of the rupture but rather one of its symptoms, a sign of his times: 'Marxism exists in nineteenth-century thought like a fish in water: that is, it is unable to breathe anywhere else'.[47]

On the face of it, then, the key difference between Foucault's conception of history and Braudel's is in the former's apparent insistence that *thought* (as opposed to the material way of life) is what defines any given period. In *The Archaeology of Knowledge*, he updates the concept of the episteme to that of 'the archive', which turns his focus from thought to discourse. Here, Foucault develops a lexicon in which the written or spoken word seems to govern the rules of entire epochs. Thus, we get the 'statement-event' and the 'statement-thing'. This discursive turn in Foucault's thinking is, I would suggest, where his obsession with power begins. For him, discourse 'appears as an asset – finite, limited, desirable, useful – that has its own rules of appearance [...] an asset that [...] poses the question of power; an asset that is, by nature, the object of a struggle, a political struggle'.[48] From here, it is only a short leap to the more famous and fuller articulation of power relations that one finds in the late Foucault, and especially in *Discipline and Punish* and *The History of Sexuality, Vol. 1*.[49] For us, I think it is important to realize that it was not necessarily Foucault's obsession with power that first animated new historicists but his insistence that the locus of history is discursive, which enabled them to go beyond the ideology critique of the Althusserians and get closer to the 'touch of the real' (i.e. through anecdotes). Gallagher and Greenblatt cast him as an 'anecdotalist' and 'counterhistorian' who sought 'to bring something back to life that had been buried deep in oblivion'. From their account, they appear drawn to what they call the 'sensationalism' of Foucault's practice, palpably excited by his fragmentation of history in which 'no analytic pattern appears' and 'no narrative arises' and which 'places him [...] on the brink of thought itself'. To the reader looking for a coherent theory of history to emerge from the new historicist take on Foucault, Gallagher and Greenblatt's account is frustratingly unsatisfactory to say the least. It seems to dance around the real issues at stake in Foucault and instead opts to revel in his apparent messiness and irreconcilability as a renegade scholar; they celebrate his 'disciplinary eccentricity'. There is a playfulness in the account that is both thrilled by the performative elements of Foucault's archaeological acts and enchanted by the prospect of an incongruous history in which seemingly anything is up for grabs. This is because their aim, above all else, is to use the anecdote 'to chip away at familiar edifices and make plastered-over cracks appear [...] to discredit the old narratives and methods'; they remain 'committed to the value of the single voice, the isolated scandal, the idiosyncratic vision, the transient sketch'.[50] It should be noted that this claim of finding a messy, patternless history appears sharply at odds with the received view of new historicist practice. Graham Bradshaw, for example, when describing Greenblatt's use of Foucault, says 'in historiographical terms the old rule-centred way of doing history has been replaced by the search for "institutional strategies" and a culture's master fictions'.[51] I will return to this in Chapter 3, but for now it is enough to note that new historicism inherits Foucault's notion of a discursive history.

This is a good point at which to turn to Hayden White, whose chief move in *Metahistory* is arguably to make history itself more akin to something like literary analysis. The major trend in literary studies of historicizing literature finds its parallel in the work of White, whose work textualizes history. Indeed, he sought to uncover the 'poetics of history' using methods borrowed from literary analysis. Perhaps it is unsurprising, then, that he has proved to have far more influence on our discipline than he has on that of our colleagues in History.[52] White's key insight is to recognize that written history isn't 'true' or 'objective', but rather a construction by historians:

> Many historians continue to treat their 'facts' as though they were 'given' and refuse to recognize, unlike most scientists, that they are not so much 'found' as 'constructed' by the kinds of questions which the investigator asks of the phenomena before him.[53]

The historian not only selects evidence and fills in the gaps but also places emphasis on certain events, privileges certain individuals, and uses a whole host of *narrative* conventions to tell a story about what happened. Indeed, the answer that I gave earlier to the question, 'What is history?, might very well have been written by White. In *Metahistory*, he takes a lot of this further by breaking down historical practice into sixteen different 'modes' (four each for 'emplotment', 'explanation', 'ideology' and 'trope'). I do not think it is necessary for our purposes to go into the details, what is important is White's notion that history, or rather histor*ies*, are essentially just 'stories', which may or may not have happened. As Jameson pointed out, in this postmodern view of history 'the past as "referent" finds itself gradually bracketed, and then effaced altogether, leaving us with nothing but texts'.[54] It is plain to see in *Practising New Historicism*, despite all their talk of the 'touch of the real', that Gallagher and Greenblatt conceive of history not only in discursive terms but also (and almost entirely, in fact) in textual terms. They are drawn to Foucault's 'fragmented and miniature stories', just as 'the indisciplined anecdote appealed to those of us who wanted to interrupt the Big Stories'. Hayden White provides the theoretical underpinning that allows literary critics such as Gallagher and Greenblatt to approach history as a set of stories, which, of course, being literary critics, they have the tools to analyse. You can see why G. R. Elton might have been banging his head against the wall at the prospect of these 'amateurs' trampling all over his turf. White gave new historicists virtual *carte blanche* to use history as a kind of literary playground in which they could employ 'outlandish and irregular [stories] [...] seemingly ephemeral details, overlooked anomalies, suppressed anachronisms' in the service of undermining 'epochal truths'.[55] New historicism's key move, then, was not to bring history to literature, but rather to make history *itself* literature. In Louis Montrose' classic dictum, it concerns itself with 'the historicity of texts and the textuality of history'.[56] It is much less a case of reading literature through the lens of history than it is seeing history through the eyes of a literary critic. There is, one might say, a certain self-contained and self-justifying satisfaction in the fact that it just so happens that the tools of literary analysis are those best suited for picking through the textual shards of history.

Later, Montrose was to articulate more fully the extent to which he meant this:

> Integral to any genuinely new historicist project [...] must be the realization and acknowledgement that our analyses and our understandings necessarily proceed from our own

> historically, socially, and institutionally shaped vantage points. As scholars, we reconstruct the past, but the versions of the past so reconstructed are also the texts that we, as historically sited subjects, have actively fashioned. Thus, a historical criticism that seeks to recover meanings that are in any final or absolute sense authentic, correct, and complete is in pursuit of an illusion.[57]

This is the complete overturn of a positivist-objectivist history for an avowedly functionalist-subjectivist history; new historicism thus formulated is the near-total antithesis of the historical approach for which the likes of Elton stood and fought. We can see in this statement the clear influence of White. The true facts of history are seen to be unknowable, because they are always-already mediated by someone whose present concerns cannot help but be registered in his or her account. Harold Aram Veeser, generally a supporter of new historicism, calls this tendency new historicism's 'narcissistic and specular loops'.[58] I do not think Veeser intends this remark disapprovingly: the new historicist and his or her contingent move as the guiding principle, for their historical materials are ever-visible, and in making those moves they cannot help but see glimpses of themselves in their subject. Elton would argue that this approach to the past is willingly anachronistic and unhistorical, and, indeed, such an argument was the point of departure for Brian Vickers' infamous rant against new historicism.[59] But in such an argument we reach an impasse. One the one hand, there are those (like Vickers) who hold that, although the past is mediated by present concerns, truths are still fundamentally knowable, and meaning is, even if imperfect, to some extent stable; and, on the other, those truly post-structuralist thinkers (like Montrose) who see such claims to the 'truth' as being so endlessly frustrated as to be futile. Howard Felperin, never less than incredibly perceptive, characterizes this as the struggle between 'conventionalism' and 'realism', but concludes, 'until some deliverance from this dilemma is found, I am afraid the best we can do is acknowledge that we are caught in it'.[60]

Having thus, through White, textualized history, the next move is to textualize all of culture itself, and this is where the influence of Clifford Geertz's anthropology is most marked. For Gallagher and Greenblatt:

> Geertz's account of the project of social science rebounded with force upon literary critics like us in the mid-1970s: it made sense of something we were already doing, returning our own professional skills to us as more important, more vital, and illuminating, than we had ourselves grasped [...] [W]e were excited to find a sophisticated intellectually powerful, and wonderfully eloquent anthropologist who could make use of the tools in our disciplinary kit and in so doing renew in us a sense of their value.[61]

Once again, the motivation appears a bit self-serving, and they characterize Geertz, as they do Foucault, as telling 'little stories'.[62] Geertz, of course, was a staunch anti-humanist, but it seems that the new historicists were less interested in his insistence that human beings are almost entirely products of their culture than in his view that culture 'is an ensemble of texts, themselves ensembles, which the anthropologist strains to read over the shoulders of those to whom they properly belong'.[63] Geertz's commitment to 'thick description', reading cultures *in situ*, and to 'local knowledge', in my view, mirror the sorts of readings that a formalist literary critic, perhaps from the school of New Criticism, might read a poem in 'reassuringly familiar terms'.[64] What is interesting for the purposes of the current study is that it is *for this explicit reason* that the new historicists embraced him to the extent they did. Gallagher and Greenblatt make the link themselves: 'Part of Geertz's power was his ability to suggest that the multi-layered cultural meanings by which he was fascinated were present in the fragments themselves, just as the literary criticism of William Empson or Kenneth Burke managed to suggest that the dense ambiguities and ironies were present in the literary texts themselves and not only in the acts of interpretation'.[65] The actual truth of Geertz's studies is of much less interest to the new historicists than the strength of his interpretative power and his view that culture is an 'acted document [...] [an] imaginative universe within which [particular] acts are signs'.[66] He allowed them to count virtually any cultural object as a 'text'. And this thinking lies behind the new historicist dismantling of traditional literary privilege. Whether the object is a Shakespeare play, a map, a bowl, a portrait of the Queen, it does not matter, they all exist as cultural markers or symbols; they are all 'texts' and, accordingly, they can be analysed as texts.

As we edge towards a new historicist 'theory of history', so we come to a natural conclusion. Like Braudel, new historicists seek to challenge the grand narratives that have been pushed by traditional history, but, unlike him, despite their calling for 'the touch of the real', they do not focus on the material practice of everyday life. Instead, their view of history, following both Foucault and White, is textual – made up of stories. And, following Geertz, their view of culture is also textual – once again, made up of stories. Not all these stories cohere towards a single unity, rather they are disparate and contradictory: they tell no single tale. And new historicists revel in that very incoherence. Through anecdotes, by highlighting peculiar and outlying instances that do not fit easily into the standard narratives, they can expose the fact that traditional history has suppressed voices that have been silent for years. It seems to me that new historicists appear not to care particularly for the question of *the truth* – that is, what 'actually happened' – because, in true post-modern fashion, they do not believe in any single stable truth. The past is always-already constructed, always-already textual, and therefore, to some extent, always-already fictional. This belies, too, their extraordinary distrust of science (inherited from Foucault). As a theory of history, it is perhaps not one we would recognize from a lay understanding of the word 'history', because it is 'built on assumptions that directly challenge the empiricist paradigm'.[67] There is missing almost entirely the will to find evidence from primary sources – the sort which G. R. Elton demanded of his 'professional' historian, and which we still find in Braudel[68] – to get to the bottom of any given matter or even to discover what took place. This aspect of new historicist thinking seems curiously self-serving. The 'point' of the new historicist essay is not to demonstrate the 'truth', or 'what happened', but rather to show off how a quirky or obscure anecdote, found as if by accident, might reveal some characteristic of the historical and cultural period – and indeed literary work from that period – that had been previously overlooked. And because of this there is a certain ironic and self-knowing playfulness in new historicist essays, especially those by Greenblatt, that almost winks at the reader as if to say 'yes, these links I'm making seem somewhat arbitrary and it is clear that I am the one weaving the pieces of this story together, but ... aren't I clever'. I do not say this to poke fun, but rather to recognize that there is a kind of postmodern celebration of critic-as-creator that lies at the heart of much new historicist practice and for which it is frequently praised.[69] Jameson calls this performative aspect of new historicism the mode of *Darstellung*, 'that sense of breathlessness, of admiration for the brilliance of the performance, but yet bewilderment, at the conclusion of the essay, from which one seems to emerge with empty hands – without ideas and interpretations to carry away with us'.[70] In a positively giddy account of Greenblatt's essay on Marlowe, from *Renaissance Self-Fashioning*, Veeser praises its 'penchant for playful, aggressive forgetfulness'.[71] New historicism does not claim to shed new light on old texts through contextualization, but, rather, purports to free up the imaginative literary critic to take the fragments of history and patch together his or her own montage of 'little stories' with which to beguile the reader.

In Chapter 3 I will return to some of the claims made by this 'theory of history' and compare them with actual new historicist practice. However, before that in Chapter 4 it will be necessary to gain a fuller understanding of new historicism's forerunners from within Shakespeare studies itself, for it could not be clearer from Gallagher and Greenblatt's account that they very much self-identified as literary critics and as coming firmly from within the discipline. New historicism has never been hostile to English or literary studies, as British cultural materialism often has, and the clue is perhaps in the speed of its assimilation in the United States. Since it is not a clean break with what came before it, then, there is surely something to be learned about the nature of new historicism in returning to that material.

2

After Tillyard, before Greenblatt

'What is New Historicism?', asks Lisa Hopkins in her *Beginning Shakespeare*, 'and what distinguishes it from "old" historicism? A good example of "old" historicism is provided by E. M. W. Tillyard'.[1] One of the unfortunate consequences of the relentless will to anthologize and summarize new historicism in critical companions, student guides and introductions has been that all too often Tillyard is ultimately the *only* representative of the supposed 'old' historicism. And I do not blame Hopkins for invoking his name as her example: it makes for the neatest narrative – *The Elizabethan World Picture* is easy to understand, the students 'get it' – and new historicism is difficult enough to grasp without complicating things further by problematizing 'old' historicism, especially not in the space of the few pages available to her. It is also true that both new historicists and cultural materialists had a habit of using Tillyard as their chief example of the bad old literary history against which they were defined. In one of the more insightful moments in his invective-laced polemic against both schools, Graham Bradshaw points out:

> As 'liberal humanists' go Tillyard was markedly illiberal and politically reactionary; those 'humanists' who had already done the critical demolition work would not spring

> to his defense, and Tillyard could not defend himself since he was dead – the perfect candidate. He had only to be exhumed, propped up on his horse like El Cid, and sent back into the field.[2]

Robin Headlam Wells, another polemical opponent of new historicism – who had, in 1985, published an excellent article, wittily entitled 'The Fortunes of Tillyard', which gives a very full picture of how Tillyard was repudiated in the 1950s, 1960s and 1970s[3] – makes the same point more emphatically:

> By the 1970s, opposition to Tillyard's view of Shakespeare's history plays as dramatic expressions of an establishment doctrine of order had become the new orthodoxy. It is puzzling, therefore, that when cultural materialists and new historicists began to reinterpret Shakespeare in the 1980s, they claimed they were rescuing criticism from a tradition that was still imprisoned by Tillyard's wartime view of Shakespeare. Since it was Tillyard and his American contemporary Lily B. Campbell who had first suggested that a study of Shakespeare's chronicle sources might illuminate the plays, this would seem to contradict the claim that pre-Theoretical criticism had ignored Shakespeare's historical context.[4]

Brian Vickers, yet another polemical opponent, makes the same point: Tillyard is 'a rather safe target, which may be attacked without danger'.[5] Although hardly impartial observers, in this case they are right: Tillyard was and still is a convenient straw man, not least because everyone has read him or encountered him at some point. He 'became prescribed reading for a generation of students', and is 'rival to A. C. Bradley in the number of well-thumbed copies of his books on today's university shelves.'[6] Michael Taylor offers some explanations for 'the secret of his immense success': 'a plain man speaking about another plain man to other plain men'. J. W. Lever was less kind: 'Tillyard's gift for bland exposition made his book more celebrated than the prim, more erudite work of [J. E.] Phillips [Jr.], but glossed over many anomalies'. Given Tillyard's obvious shortcomings, Taylor later wonders, about 'the neglect by the new historicists and cultural materialists of Wilbur Sanders, Robert Ornstein, J. W. Lever, Jan Kott, A. P. Rossiter, Norman Rabkin, and so on – anti-Tillyard to a man'.[7]

Wells, meanwhile, continues to hammer the point home: 'The assertion that it was Theory that rescued Shakespeare criticism from Tillyard's "monological approach" was to become a defining principle of cultural-materialist and new-historicist apologetics'. In a forensically damning passage that reads not unlike a headmaster rebuking a set of pupils for failing to hand in their homework, Wells points to eight instances of contemporary critics (Jonathan Dollimore, Barbara Hodgson, Hugh Grady, John Drakakis, John Joughin, Andrew Hadfield, Ewan Fernie and Ramona Wray) making exactly this assertion. 'The Tudor Myth had been replaced by the Tillyard Myth', he argues. 'To claim that it was Theory that taught us to read Shakespeare in his historical context, and that it was Theory that revealed that literary texts might be open to a number of interpretations, is to ignore a central strand in twentieth-century criticism'.[8] Once again, Wells is correct on this score: the oft-repeated claim – now virtually received wisdom in the discipline – that new historicism and cultural materialism rescued Shakespeare studies from the twin evils of Tillyard and New Criticism is a fiction created for the convenience of tidy narrative.

In this chapter, I am going to problematize the received view of 'old' historicism by focusing on the sort of literary history in Shakespeare studies that was being written after Tillyard but before Greenblatt's *Renaissance Self-Fashioning* in 1980.[9] This is, roughly speaking, the period from the 1950s to the 1970s in which one would expect to find the landscape dominated by New Critics.[10] I seek to overturn what Douglas Bruster calls 'inadequate generalizations about previous scholarship'.[11] The first thing to note is that 'old' historicism is a retroactive label that has been created for the express purpose of defining new historicism. As Ann Baynes Coiro and Thomas Fulton put it, 'there was never any such thing as "Old Historicism" – no one ever called him- or herself an Old Historicist, or set up a sign denoting such a school for others to join'.[12] Second, the idea that adherents to New Criticism refused to look at historical context at all is or that it was steadfastly 'dominant' until 1980, like much of the standard narrative, is at best a drastic over-simplification, and at worst a complete falsehood. The refusal to look at context is perhaps true of Cleanth Brooks, whose *Well Wrought Urn* (1947) is invoked almost as much as Tillyard for the purposes of straw-manning. It may also be true to some extent of certain critics who focused squarely on Shakespeare's language, such as B. Ifor Evans, Frank Kermode, M. M. Mahood or James Calderwood – although even they would take time to outline Shakespeare's 'learning' and classical allusions. However, I think it is fair to say that formalism peaked in Shakespeare studies a decade before Brooks, with Caroline Spurgeon's *Shakespeare's Imagery and What It Tells Us* (1935) and the maverick works of G. Wilson Knight. The majority of Shakespearean critics after the war combined close textual reading with historical scholarship, and I would include among their number liberal humanist advocates of Shakespeare's studied ambiguity, such as William Empson, Norman Rabkin and A. P. Rossiter.[13] Jürgen Pieters astutely makes this very point: 'While in the past, there have been a number of fierce polemics between representatives of traditional historicism and the formalist advocates of New Criticism [...] the history of Shakespeare studies suggests that both paradigms were largely compatible'.[14] They retained the capacity, as G. K. Hunter put it, 'to be both historical and formalist [...] to see Shakespeare as a child of his age, yet to assess his works as independent creations which speak [...] to any age.'[15] Hence, we find strange cases, such as John Dover Wilson, who might be evoked as an example of a New Critic in one place and as an 'old' historicist in another.[16] Even L. C. Knights, so frequently cited as a Leavisite and a member of the *Scrutiny* school, produced a work of literary history that is practically Marxist in its commitment to viewing Ben Jonson in his socio-economic context.[17]

Let us not labour the point. My purpose here is to take some time to consider some historicist studies written between 1940s and 1970s that pre-figure new historicism. There are four key studies in this respect: Francis Fergusson's *The Idea of Theater* (1949), C. L. Barber's *Shakespeare's Festive Comedies* (1959), Wilbur Sanders's *The Dramatist and the Received Idea* (1968) and Stephen Orgel's *The Illusion of Power* (1975).[18] I will also give special mention to J. W. Lever's essay 'Shakespeare and the Ideas of his Time' (1976), which will be a constant reference point. Lever's own book, *The Tragedy of State* (1971) might also have been included, but, since he deals with non-Shakespearean texts it must be relegated to the background. We think of studies like these as being 'pre-theory', but what that really means is 'pre-French Theory of a particular stripe'. As we shall see, this work is neither un-theoretical nor free from outside influences. And this has perhaps been another consequence of new historicism's flattening of the critical past: it is too often assumed that criticism before 1980 was unreflectively 'essentialist humanist', which not only does a disservice to past critics but also muddies the view of those trying to gain a clear sense of the academic climate from which new historicism arose.[19] I am not going to read these texts exhaustively for their specific arguments, but, rather, in keeping with my overall aims I want to gain a sense of what 'theory of history' is at play in each of them and how new historicism's own conception of history compares. For this it will be necessary to do some intellectual excavation.

Between Fergusson and Barber we can draw a clear link: the anthropologist James George Frazer, whose epic and sprawling *The Golden Bough* (1890) traces the history of pagan religions and festivals from 'primitive man' through antiquity to the medieval period; it also proved influential to Northrop Frye. By its third edition it had twelve volumes.

Such far-reaching anthropological studies were *en vogue* at the turn of the century, as we might witness by taking a glance at Friedrich Engels' *The Origin of the Family, Private Property and the State* (1884) and Edward Westermarck's two books, *The History of Human Marriage* (1891) and *The Origin and Development of the Moral Ideas* (1906).[20] Here, the impact and influence of Charles Darwin's theory of evolution can be felt everywhere. In these studies we can trace the development of modern sociology – indeed Westermarck was the first professor of that discipline in the United Kingdom, one year after Émile Durkheim in France. Within his own field, Frazer suffered a decline in reputation during his own lifetime, and by the time of his death in 1941 it was 'dismal'.[21] His work was finally overturned by the functionalism of Bronisław Malinowski, who, while being a professed fan, complained of his 'piecemeal treatments of isolated items'.[22] Despite that, Frazer's *Golden Bough* found a mainstream audience (at least among educated readers), and was by turn controversial and popular. It was enormously influential in the field of classics, and it was an inspiration to modernist writers, especially T. S. Eliot.[23] Frazer was also somewhat influential in psychology, on Carl Jung's idea of the collective unconscious, of course, and especially in the area of the incest taboo. Frazer is a frequently used touchstone in Sigmund Freud's *Totem and Taboo* (1913), and some of his ideas about taboos have proved influential in modern evolutionary psychology, especially in the work of Steven Pinker and Jonathan Haidt.[24] Broadly speaking, there was a split in anthropology between rationalist cultural evolutionists such as Frazer and Westermarck, who believed in the idea of human progress from an earlier more 'primitive' state to modernity and who tended to focus on the (general) psychology of individuals in cultures, and Durkheim who insisted that individuals are socially determined. In Durkheim culture perpetuates itself through collective myths, rituals, and sacred symbols – the very same that Frazer had so exhaustively gathered in his data collections. Durkheim prevailed, and the symbolic approach became the more dominant in the twentieth century. We can draw a direct line from Durkheim to Claude Lévi-Strauss, who was his student, and to Clifford Geertz, who, as I mentioned briefly earlier, set himself up against Lévi-Strauss.

As a staunch rationalist, Frazer believed, adapting the Darwinian idea of evolutionary progress, that human beings had three distinct stages of development: the first is a belief in magic and superstition; the second, a belief in religion; the third, in science. For him 'The history of religion is a long attempt to reconcile old custom with new reason, to find sound theory for an absurd practice'.[25] In *The Golden Bough*, he set himself the task of finding patterns of similarity – archetypes – in religious rituals and practices through history and across cultures. We can see here how this Victorian brand of anthropology, much more interested in 'broad trans-cultural sweep',[26] would be at odds with later anthropology's focus on particularity and 'local knowledge'. Frazer's insistence on his three stages perhaps does a disservice to the level of detail in his work, which is piled high with footnotes: he would sooner give twenty examples of a particular rite or ritual than just one. But the way in which he ranges from one example to the other has something of the flavour of the *Annales* school about it, and indeed, he was an early influence on Marc Bloch.[27] Perhaps his key legacy, however, was in influencing the so-called Cambridge Ritualists, led by Jane Ellen Harrison, a fascinating figure in her own right.[28] They did not follow his view of the stages of development, but they did come to see myth and ritual as being inextricably linked and as being a type of human universal. And it is from here that we can trace the intellectual journey into literary criticism. As Stanley Edgar Hyman – a great chronicler of literary critical trends after the war and a literary theorist of sorts himself – argued in 1962:

> In the work of [...] the Cambridge Ritualists – Harrison, Francis Cornford, and A. B. Cook – the influence of Frazer permanently transformed and revitalized the field of

> classics [...] The application of these ideas from classical to medieval to modern literature by a brilliant series of literary critics – William Troy, Francis Fergusson, Herbert Weisinger, John Speirs, C. L. Barber and others – has given Frazer an importance in literary criticism at least equal to that of Marx and Freud.[29]

While this might seem overblown today, what Patricia Waugh calls 'literary anthropology' and what is listed in Oscar James Campbell's *Shakespeare Encyclopaedia* as 'mythic criticism' was very influential in the 1940s and 1950s.[30] Its originator was Maud Bodkin, but, both within and outside Shakespeare studies, its torchbearer was Northrop Frye.[31] It is a heady mix of myth-ritual analysis, Jungian psychology, archetypes and the sort of pattern-spotting that was popular with more formalist critics such as Spurgeon or Wilson Knight. Frye remained committed to finding universals, and this is reflected in his thinking on Shakespeare. In his view, Shakespeare 'establish[es] contact with a universal and worldwide dramatic tradition' by drawing 'away from everything that is local or specialized in the drama of his day', and working 'towards uncovering the primeval dramatic structure that practically anything in the shape of a human audience can respond to'.[32]

While these developments were taking shape, Francis Fergusson was at the forefront of the bid to take in influences from other disciplines. 'At this point', he says, 'the studies of historians, theologians, and anthropologists are useful, for they may help to free us from some of our provincial habits of mind'. In *The Idea of Theater*, Fergusson acknowledges his indebtedness to 'the Cambridge School, Fraser [*sic*], Cornford, Harrison, Murray', but only directly cites any of them (Harrison) once in the whole book.[33] This belies the fact that Fergusson deals mostly in generalities rather than specificities: he is looking to establish broad and generalized rules about theatre as ritual forms as a launch pad for his textual analyses. Although he was to publish a whole book on Shakespeare later – *Shakespeare: The Pattern in His Carpet*

(1970)[34] – *The Idea of Theater* contains a single chapter on *Hamlet* in a study that ranges from classical plays, such as *Oedipus Rex*, to Ibsen and Chekov.

In that chapter, he argues against Ernest Jones' famous Freudian reading of the play and the prevailing view that it is about its protagonist's introspection.[35] To understand a play like *Hamlet*, Fergusson insists, we must understand 'the whole idea of the theater which Shakespeare used and assumed in his audience'. For Fergusson:

> [O]n stage, the music and drums and the marching of royal and military pageantry, are directly absorbing, and they assure us that something of great and general significance is going on. From time to time the stage is emptied; the pageantry is gone; the stories seem to be marking time – and Hamlet emerges, alone, or with one or two interlocutors. Sometimes he suffers his visions before us; sometimes he makes jokes and topical allusions; sometimes he spars with his interlocutors like the gag-man in a minstrel show, or the master of ceremonies in a modern musical.[36]

Fergusson argues that the play oscillates between ritual and improvisation, depending on the scene. He also claims that Shakespeare's theatre had a 'central place in society' which allowed it to reflect the values of that society directly as 'the central mirror of the life of its times'.[37] Citing Tillyard, and his chief source, Arthur O. Lovejoy,[38] he points out that the very structure of the Elizabethan playhouse reflected the belief in the Great Chain of Being, with its painted canopy representing heaven. Fergusson's main argument is that, in its centrality and close symbolic mirroring of everyday beliefs, 'the Elizabethan theater must be regarded as the heir to Greek tragic theater with its ritual basis [...] Shakespeare's theater is thus akin to the theater of Sophocles'.[39] It should be seen, first and foremost, as being communal. There is a lot in Fergusson's work that bears virtually no relation to new historicism: not least his constant need to draw trans-historical and trans-cultural patterns across these plays, his apparently straight-forward acceptance of the Tillyard doctrine, and in his humanist assumption that drama can get us closer to the 'mystery of human life'. However, in his insistence on situating Shakespeare's plays in its theatre setting, in his willingness to bring anthropological studies and mythologies to bear in literary analysis, and in his broader view that plays represent a glimpse of the societies that produced them in microcosm, we can at least see some of the directions that new historicism would later take.

C. L. Barber has undoubtedly been more influential than Fergusson. Partly, this is because he was primarily a scholar of Shakespeare and the early modern period, and did not range across the discipline's periodical boundaries as Fergusson did. Partly, this is because he has been avowed as a key influence by Stephen Greenblatt himself, who in 1985 contributed a version of 'Invisible Bullets' to a collection of essays published in his honour,[40] and later wrote the foreword for a reprint of *Shakespeare's Festive Comedy*. Partly, this is because that study has proved to be a seminal text in affording Shakespeare's comedies serious attention alongside the tragedies – Fergusson's reading of *Hamlet* would not rank in a hypothetical top twenty most important essays on that play, whereas Barber's readings of *As You Like It* and *Twelfth Night* would be near the top of the reading lists from both those plays. But, mostly, it is because *Shakespeare's Festive Comedy* is a leap forward in terms of its historical scholarship. Barber has none of Fergusson's more grandstanding tendencies, and the latter's generalizations give way to detail. Barber uses Frazer more as repository of information than as a theoretical guide: he is little more than a source for details of obscure ceremonies. There is a nod to Frye early on,[41] but one never gets the sense that Barber is trying to put forward any great theory of drama, or of Shakespeare's works, beyond pointing out their partial basis in 'Saturnalian' festive rituals. G. K. Hunter even complained that it was too piecemeal, and, perhaps unsurprisingly, it is this very quality that Greenblatt so admires: 'the subtlety and evident delight with which he weaves together aptly chosen snippets of social and cultural history'.[42] One can plainly see Greenblatt positioning Barber as a forerunner of his own practice.

Barber argues that comedies on the Elizabethan stage are the 'civilized equivalent of the primitive rite'.[43] But the phrase 'equivalent of', here, must not be mistaken for 'is', it functions only on the level of analogy, because the Elizabethan era was not 'primitive'. In this respect, Barber marks a break both with Fergusson, who as we saw, was at pains to point out how similar Elizabethan theatre was to its classical forebears, and with Frye, of whose ideas about universality he appears sceptical. Consider the following passage:

> One way in which our time has been seeing the universal in literature has been to find in complex literary works patterns which are analogous to myths and rituals and which can be regarded as archetypes, in some sense primitive or fundamental. I have found this approach very exciting indeed. But at the same time, such analysis can be misleading if it results in equating the literary form with primitive analogues [...] Shakespeare was the opposite of primitivistic, for in his culture what we search out and call primitive was in the blood and bone as a matter of course; the problem was to deal with it, to master it. The Renaissance, moreover, was a moment when educated men were modifying a ceremonial conception of human life to create a historical conception. The ceremonial view, which assumed that names and meanings are fixed and final, expressed experience as pageant and ritual – pageant where the right names could march in proper order, or ritual where names could be changed in the right, the proper way. The historical view expresses life as drama [...] [in which] pageants are regularly interrupted; the rituals are abortive or perverted; or if they succeed, they succeed against odds or in an unexpected fashion. The people in plays try to

organize their lives by pageant and ritual, but the plays are dramatic precisely because the effort fails.[44]

Barber's argument about these attempts at ritualization failing is more radical than it might first appear:[45] it is not only a break with Fergusson and Frye but also from the Tillyardian view that Elizabethan theatre reflected at all times the Great Chain of Being. Barber finds quite the reverse: that drama fundamentally depends on attempts to impose order on human life breaking down. For him, 'Shakespeare's drama can be seen as part of the process by which our culture has moved from absolutist modes of thought towards a historical and psychological view of man'.[46]

It is perhaps surprising therefore, that so often in his readings, Barber's conclusions are essentially conservative. For Barber, the 'saturnalian' festive form that Elizabethan pleasure so often took had built into it a final acceptance of everyday norms once carnival conditions were over. Carnival allows a period of virtually unrestrained freedom and 'misrule', but like all holidays it must come to an end, and people have to go back to work. He calls this process 'release' (the period of carnival) and 'clarification' (the world as it is in normal conditions), of which 'kill-joys' – such as Shylock from *The Merchant of Venice* and Malvolio from *Twelfth Night*, 'the butts in the festive plays' – are constant reminders. 'In the actual observance of customary misrule, the control of the disruptive motives which the festivity expresses is achieved by the group's recognition of the place of the whole of business within the larger rhythm of their continuing social life'.[47] We can see in this the genesis of Greenblatt's famed subversion-containment model. Freedom and subversion are glimpsed in the comedies, only ultimately to reinforce the status quo. In *Shakespearean Negotiations* (1988), Greenblatt builds his reading of *Twelfth Night* virtually on top of Barber's. He quotes Barber directly: 'The most fundamental distinction the play brings home to us is the difference between men and women [...] Just as the saturnalian reversal of social roles need not threaten the social structure, but can instead serve to consolidate it, so a temporary, playful reversal of sexual roles can renew the meaning of the normal relation'.[48] Greenblatt finds, almost identically, that, in *Twelfth Night*, 'we learn that the threat to social order and the threat to sexual order were equally illusory. All's well that ends well'.[49] We can see here how it is possible to break with the Tillyard doctrine but still see Shakespeare as being a conservative playwright.

Before leaving Barber, however, it is worth pointing out that he and Greenblatt diverge significantly on the topic of Falstaff and the *Henry IV* plays. In arguably his most famous essay, 'Invisible Bullets', Greenblatt finds:

> The subversive voices [in *The Henriad*] are produced by and within the affirmations of order; they are powerfully registered, but they do not undermine that order [...] Shakespeare refuses to endorse so baldly cynical a conception of the social order [as Falstaff's]; instead actions that should have the effect of radically undermining authority turn out to be the props of that authority [...] We are invited to take measure of [Henry IV's] suffering, to understand [...] the costs of power. And we are invited to understand those costs in order to ratify the power, to accept the grotesque and cruelly unequal distribution of possessions: everything to the few, nothing to the many [...] The play appears to ratify the established order, with the new-crowned Henry V merging his body into 'the great body of our state', with Falstaff despised and rejected.[50]

Here, Greenblatt sees Shakespeare siding with state power against Falstaff. Barber, on the other hand, sees Falstaff as being a personification of carnival, who is put on 'trial' in *2 Henry IV*. He postulates that, in trying to solve the 'problem' of Falstaff's attitude by shipping him off, Shakespeare fails in justifying the dramatic action. 'The trouble with trying to get rid of this attitude merely by getting rid of Falstaff', Barber argues, 'is that the attitude is too pervasive in the whole society of the play, whether public or private'.[51] There is something in the festive spirit as manifest in Falstaff that Barber seems to be suggesting, implicitly, is intrinsically human. 'Banish plump Jack, and banish all the world' (*1 Henry IV*, 2.4.397–8). We can see in this difference between Greenblatt's and Barber's responses to Falstaff's rejection a broader trend between new historicists and their immediate predecessors that we shall see repeated time and again: very often it is the new historicist position that is the more orthodox and the more conservative.

This is certainly the case when we look at the critical reception of the history plays from the 1950s to the 1970s. J. W. Lever, writing in 1976, shows how providential 'Tudor myth' readings by Tillyard and his contemporaries[52] were overturned in twenty years:

> [I]t was Shakespeare's politics that received most scholarly attention during the years that culminated in the second world war. In no other field of thought was his conformity to received ideas so often proclaimed, or his 'fixed' and 'consistent' beliefs so confidently declared [...] [By the end of the 1960s] a transformed conception of Shakespeare's creative processes was beginning to take shape. In important respects it was a return to the intuitive outlook of the early years of the century. Shakespeare's humanism, his freedom from dogmas, his inherently dramatic approach, were again being affirmed. But in the rejection of a blinkered historicism some more definitive insights had been gained.[53]

At the transition point Lever identifies, we can find what is probably the most systematic dismantling of Tillyard's view of Shakespeare's histories (as conforming to a providential view of history) in Wilbur Sanders's *The Dramatist and the Received Idea*. Although Lever argues that Sanders was fighting a battle that had 'already been fought',[54] from today's vantage point it reads more like the final victory of liberal humanist scholarship over the 'old' historicism of Tillyard than an after-note.

The study is not without its flaws, however: Sanders pits Shakespeare against Christopher Marlowe and sets out to analyse the ways in which both dramatists employed the 'received ideas' of their time. In this he makes a number of value judgements. He finds typically that Shakespeare makes very good use of received ideas, because he genuinely explores and interrogates them. Shakespeare creates 'a dramatic environment and a philosophical climate in which the threshold of orthodoxy is lowered and the mind is free to play over a wider range of possibilities than would otherwise be available to it'. It is a version of the Empson or Rossiter view of Shakespeare-as-Janus: the ambivalent playwright, writing at a moment of cultural transition, who can always look in two directions at once and consider all possibilities without imposing a particular conclusion.[55] Marlowe, on the other hand, is much less successful, for a variety of reasons; typically, where Shakespeare is subtle and nuanced, Marlowe is heavy-handed. Sanders finds Marlowe altogether too enamoured of a crude version of Machiavelli, and so *The Jew of Malta* becomes 'brutality masquerading as realism', and *Edward II* 'no more than the reporter's realism, the kind which finally shrinks a whole dimension of the real – the moral'. Even *Doctor Faustus*, for Sanders, is 'disordered' and 'hectic', 'a sadly imperfect monument to a gifted dramatist who never really finished anything' – although the question of why Marlowe's inability to make up his mind is seen as confused while Shakespeare's refusal to draw stable conclusions is praised is left unanswered.[56] This moralistic approach, wedded to a tendency to build Shakespeare up by tearing Marlowe down, is unfortunate, and it is what most dates the work when read today.

However, the great value of Sanders – and the reason to go back to him – lies in his willingness to go beyond standard or orthodox sources. He seeks to consider a full range of influential ideas at play in the Elizabethan milieu beyond the official doctrine, including those of Niccolò Machiavelli, John Calvin, Thomas Aquinas and Richard Hooker. He is at his best when exposing the one-dimensionality of 'old' historicist scholarship.

> [There] is more to be said about the political orthodoxy which is, in Professor [Lily B.] Campbell's disquisition, a mere fixed point of reference. It is not merely that she has assumed an extremely simple and direct relationship between Elizabethan political speculation and Shakespeare's historical *oeuvre* – even to the extent of deducing his purposes in writing the plays from current views on the political uses of history [...] like Tillyard and Ribner she has also fastened, in her exposition of 'the Tudor theory of kingship', on a single aspect of the sixteenth-century political theory – what might be called the Administration's ego-image – and labelled it 'orthodoxy'. If this designation is correct, either the Tudor propaganda machine was one of unparalleled efficiency, or else the Elizabethans were sadly deficient in independence of mind and critical awareness – neither of which was the case [...] The rarefied atmosphere of political theology is, however, only a part of the political air that Shakespeare breathed; for he wrote the history plays towards the end of a century of bitter and acrimonious debate.[57]

In this quotation we can see two distinctive features of Sanders' work: the first is a refusal to accept a monolithic view of culture, a rejection of the 'spirit of the age' or 'world picture' arguments that define the 'old' historicism of Tillyard and Campbell. He insists on registering multiple voices in the 'debate', and in this also has a keen sense of which ideas, if we are to borrow some concepts from Raymond Williams, are residual, dominant and emergent.[58] New historicism has taken something of this, although it should be noted that Sanders is still working very much in the mode of the history of *ideas*, an intellectual history, whereas new historicists, as we have seen, profess to focus on the everyday (as mediated textually). The second feature is Sanders' insistence that the people of the past were reflective and intelligent. He assumes that individuals in Shakespeare's time were able to consider a range of possibilities, and he finds the scope for multivalence even in doctrines which are assumed to be orthodox. In the former feature, we find what new historicists later claimed to have achieved: a truly heterodox view of history that is sceptical of all claims that there was a single hegemony. In the latter, however, we can see a real divergence. Sanders is a humanist, and accordingly he sees deliberate human thought everywhere. Following Foucault, individuals in new historicist thinking are generally effaced and appear to be much more un-reflective as the passive receptacles of various currents that circulate through the period. Because of this, new historicist readings of the histories actually turn out to be closer to those of 'old' historicists than to critics such as Sanders, or indeed, Rossiter, who emphasized the freedom of Shakespeare's thinking. More on this in Chapter 3.

Before we get there, let us turn briefly to Stephen Orgel's *The Illusion of Power*. This short book is a distillation of a much more substantial study: *Inigo Jones: Theatre of the Stuart Court* (1973).[59] In writing it, Orgel collaborated with the famed art historian, Roy C. Strong. The hero of the book, and of *The Illusion of Power*, is the architect Inigo Jones, who designed many theatrical masques during the reign of James I. Orgel argues that, in order to understand Jacobean theatre, we must draw a distinction between public theatre – the theatre of The Globe, for example, and even of Blackfriars – and the private theatre of the court. Also, he says, we should remember that theatre is inextricably visual, as well as verbal. What particularly interests Orgel about Jones' designs for these masques is the central and prominent position afforded to the monarch, which reflects 'the ways in which the age saw the monarchy'. 'Masques', he argues, 'were the festal embodiments of this concept of monarchy'. The crucial realization is that the members of the audience for these spectacles were not there to see the show, but rather to see the monarch themselves: 'The king must not merely see the play, he must be seen to see it. The fact that the latter requirement interferes with the former is of no consequence [...] What this audience has come to *see* is the king'. The performance of any given piece, then, in such a private court is completely indivisible from its immediate context: the 'text', as it were, is the specific event itself, 'not simply the action of the play, but the interaction between the play and monarch'.[60]

Orgel is frequently claimed to be the first new historicist, or otherwise identified with the movement. Richard Wilson, for example, writing in 1992, did not hesitate to declare *The Illusion of Power* 'one of the finest and sharpest New Historicist works'.[61] I think this might be jumping the gun a little. There is missing entirely the influence of Foucault or Geertz, or any hint of the textual view of history I outlined in Chapter 1. Orgel's approach seems to be rooted more in the stuff of the material theatre. However, his view of royal power as manifest both in the spectacle of the court performance and in the playwright's representations of it does anticipate closely the Foucault-inspired new historicism that was to come in the next decade. In *The Tempest*, for example, he finds an analogy between the power of Prospero, the power of God and the power of the king watching the masque (James I).

> Modern critics are made exceedingly uncomfortable by the idea of Prospero as God. Can Shakespeare have meant to deify a figure so arbitrary, ill-tempered, vindictive? [...] We want our God all love, our Jesus meek and mild, but [the early modern] God is, like Prospero, a god of storms and power too. As with the gods in the Renaissance, so with kings [...] What is recorded in these productions is the growth of a political ideology [...] [T]he truth of the royal productions was the truth of the appearances. Power was asserted only through analogies, faith affirmed only through symbols.[62]

As we shall see in Chapter 3, this idea of power through analogy was to prove very influential for new historicists in the 1980s, especially for Jonathan Goldberg. Claire Colebrook is very good on this point: 'Orgel was one of the first critics to see *The Tempest* as a statement about the power of art and representation. In doing so he inaugurated what became a feature of new historicist criticism: the *recognition* of new historicism's own theory in the very texts it studies'.[63] This implicitly reflects new historicism's perpetual awareness of the critic's own place in history, which denies the 'old' historicist assumption that 'history is knowable', while simultaneously recognizing 'the agency of criticism in constructing and delimiting the subject of study, and of the historical positioning of the critic *vis-à-vis* that subject; and thus a renunciation of the illusory quest of an older historical criticism to recover objective, authentic, or stable "meanings"'.[64]

In this chapter, we have seen how new historicism was anticipated in several respects, during the 1950s, 1960s and 1970s, by the post-Tillyard practice of literary history in Shakespeare studies, although with important and significant differences. In Fergusson and Barber, we see the willingness to incorporate findings and methods from anthropology and sociology. Of course, later, the point of departure for new historicists was anthropology – Geertz rather than Frazer or the Cambridge Ritualists – and, with the change of influence, so we see a change in the underlying theoretical assumptions. New historicists also inherit Barber's commitment to seeing Shakespeare's comedies as borrowing elements from pagan rites and festivals, which challenges and complicates the monolithic view of Shakespeare's time that we get from Tillyard and others. However, despite this, Barber's readings of Shakespeare's plays are very often conservative, because he sees the 'Saturnalian' elements as being temporal, a glimpse at the carnival, and working ultimately to reinforce the norms of the status quo. Barber, therefore, sees Shakespeare as working almost always to contain the scope for genuine subversion, and new historicists have largely followed him in this respect.

In Sanders we see a genuinely heterodox account of ideas and beliefs in Shakespeare's period – perhaps to an extent that we do not see replicated in new historicism. However, his practice differs from new historicism in two crucial respects. First, he is concerned with an intellectual history: the history of ideas, rather than of the 'everyday' or 'the real'. Second, as a liberal humanist, Sanders assumes that individuals maintain a certain independence of mind from their time and place to an extent that new historicists do not seem to entertain or allow. Finally, in Orgel we find the nearest forebear to new historicism: a close attention to Shakespeare's immediate theatrical context in London wedded to an analysis of monarchical power as manifest in James I's court. However, Orgel is lacking many of the theoretical underpinnings defined in Chapter 1. We do not see explicit in his work the postmodern view of history as being textual, even if there is something of the postmodern unknowability of history in the fact that he sees his own theories about power reflected in Shakespeare's plays. In the next chapter, we will see how Orgel's ideas about power were developed by new historicists in the 1980s.

3

Power, Containment and Cultural Poetics

It is ebb and flow, tidal gravity! It is ecological balance! You are an old man who thinks in terms of nations and peoples. There are no nations. There are no peoples [...] There is only one holistic system of systems, one vast and immane, interwoven, interacting, multivariate, multinational dominion of dollars. Petro-dollars, electro-dollars, multi-dollars, reichmarks, rins, rubles, pounds, and shekels. It is the international system of currency which determines the totality of life on this planet [...] The world is a college of corporations, inexorably determined by the immutable bylaws of business. The world is a business [...] It has been since man crawled out of the slime [...] One vast and ecumenical holding company [...] in which all men will hold a share of stock. All necessities provided, all anxieties tranquilized, all boredom amused. (Arthur Jensen, *Network*, 1975)

But what is 'social energy'? The term implies something measurable, yet I cannot provide a convenient and reliable formula for isolating a single, stable quantum for examination. We identify *energia* only indirectly, by its effects [...] [T]here is no originary moment, no pure act of untrammelled creation. In place of a blazing genesis, one begins to

> glimpse [...] a subtle, elusive set of exchanges, a network of trades and trade-offs, a jostling of competing representations, a negotiation between joint-stock companies. (Stephen Greenblatt)[1]

In Chapters 1 and 2 I came to a view of new historicism that foregrounds both the heterodoxy and textuality of history. Following Hayden White, new historicists contest a series of stable assumptions made by older historians: 'that history is knowable; that literature mirrors or at least by indirection reflects historical reality; and that historians and critics can see the facts of history objectively'.[2] Following Clifford Geertz and Michel Foucault, they also come to see culture as being fundamentally discursive or textual. It seems to me, however, that there is a disconnect between the theoretical account of new historicism I have outlined – based largely on that given by Catherine Gallagher and Stephen Greenblatt in *Practicing New Historicism*, which we must remember was written in 2000, with support from Louis Montrose' *The Purpose of Playing*, itself written in 1996 – and what new historicists *actually did* in the 1980s and 1990s. As any reader familiar with that work will already know, the emphasis on 'counterhistory' in Gallagher and Greenblatt's account is vastly overstated, not least because it is so often the case that their 'counterhistory' turns out to be a reinforcement of older orthodox readings.

It was partly this that must have infuriated G. R. Elton. We must recall that Elton was an historian who had spent his entire career fighting to overturn the idea that the Tudor state was despotic. Greenblatt and other new historicists, as we shall see, set about reinforcing the view of the despotic and absolutist Tudor state, and perhaps this is partly why Elton came to hate both them and literary theory. The historian Richard C. McCoy sums this up well:

> In the traditional view, the cult of Elizabeth [I] persisted in its flattering effusions despite the evidence of physical decline because of what Frances Yates perceives as a 'deep need

> for order' pervading sixteenth-century Europe [...] More recent accounts of the cult of Elizabeth, particularly those associated with the New Historicism, stand this idealizing view of Monarchy on its head. Michel Foucault's essentially paranoid conception of power has been immensely influential, and variations on the harrowing scenes of torture and execution in Foucault's *Discipline and Punish* feature prominently in the work of Stephen Greenblatt, Leonard Tennenhouse, Jonathan Goldberg, Steven Mullaney, and others. The result is a kind of *film noir* version of the Elizabethan world picture, starring the queen as supreme dominatrix in a courtly theatre of cruelty. While less enraptured than older views of sovereignty, these newer versions sometimes reinforce a fundamentally hegemonic and conservative idea of Court politics [...] Two decades ago, G. R. Elton set out to demolish such exalted and conservative views of the court of Elizabeth [...] [and attacked them for being] absolutist fantasies.[3]

Blair Worden, another historian, makes a similar point about the earlier Tudor period:

> The notion of a 'Tudor despotism' has suffered formidable blows from Sir Geoffrey Elton, who believes the rule of law to have prevailed in Henry's reign – or at least in the period of Thomas Cromwell's supremacy [...] Stephen Greenblatt, who, in *Renaissance Self-Fashioning*, writes so memorably on More and Wyatt, impairs his case by too easily calling Henry VIII a Stalin, for the ambitions and resources of 20th-century tyranny were beyond the imagination of Tudor England.[4]

Let me pause on Worden's final line: why in his view might Greenblatt or other new historicists 'too easily' be calling a Tudor or Stuart monarch 'a Stalin'? This is a question I want to bear in mind throughout this chapter. The suspicion that new historicism is a case of old wine in new bottles is almost as old as new historicism itself.[5] But it remains valid to wonder why the theoretical project of producing 'counterhistory' – one that supposedly opposed E. M. W. Tillyard – in practice rewound the clock to a pre-Elton account of a despotic Tudor state.

Accordingly, in this chapter I will look directly at some of the key new historicists studies from the 1980s and 1990s in order to answer two fundamental and related questions: first, since it was buttressed by radical postmodern theory which supposedly – as David Scott Kastan put it, 'is seen to attack the great tradition of Western culture [...] like the crown-of-thorns starfish ravaging the great barrier reef'[6] – how did it come to pass that the version of Shakespeare and his historical moment that we get from new historicism so often turns out to seem *more conservative* than earlier accounts that we get of the period from scholars as disparate and different as G. R. Elton and Wilbur Sanders? In other words, where is the 'counter-history' that Gallagher and Greenblatt spoke so much about in *Practising New Historicism*? Second, how do new historicists account for social change?

New historicism's apparent obsession with the representation and machinations of power has long been its most defining and enduring characteristic. Writing in 1996, Louis Montrose summed up the key controversies that distinguished new historicism's reception in its first fifteen years:

> At the center of much critical practice and polemic has been the nature and scope of the agency available to subjects of the early modern state, and the degree to which contestation of the dominant ideology and its institutions was possible and actualized. The terms in which the problematic of ideology and resistance came to be posed in Renaissance studies were those of an opposition between *subversion* and *containment*.[7](emphasis in original)

Generally, the British cultural materialism can be characterized as seeing scope for the former, whereas American new historicism saw everywhere confirmation of the latter.

In *James I and the Politics of Literature* (1983), an early new historicist study on which we need not dwell for too long (I will return to it in Chapter 4),[8] Jonathan Goldberg provides the natural theoretical bridge to and extension from Stephen Orgel's *The Illusion of Power* (1975). Orgel's emphasis on power as manifest in the spectacle of James I's court finds itself reinforced by Foucault and Geertz:

> According to Michel Foucault, sovereign power affirms itself by claiming what it enacts is outside itself and transcendent. The claim and the appeal to universal principles give language to the fact of power – that power is concomitant with might and it acts as imposition. Imposing words give power its strength.
> [...]
> Power, Geertz concludes, is not brute force; that view of power is just that – a conception of power, not a natural fact nor inherent to it. Power can be as truly in display [...] making its life a series of repeated representations of a condition best exemplified in the unmoving drama that the king presented. For the king of Bali, Geertz remarks, represented himself, theatricalized himself. And so, too, did James, in the spectacle he presented in his progress through London. What he offered was not simply an image of his power, but the power of himself as image. And such power extended from his exemplary form to embrace the entire state.[9]

Goldberg's James I is like the perfect Foucauldian dictator ruling over his subjects through a discourse which seamlessly combines royal and verbal power, the state and the court masque, the body politic and the play – as Worden might put it, he is 'a Stalin'. There is an easy, direct one-to-one relation in Goldberg between monarch, performance, text and playwright. Ben Jonson or Shakespeare are conduits for the all-powerful king reflecting back at him a representation of his own power, so that the various rulers within their plays – say,

Tiberius in *Sejanus* or the Duke in *Measure for Measure* – are analogous to James I, with the implied gaze of the audience on them reflecting their actual gaze on the real king (i.e. James) at court. Goldberg notes that sometimes the vision of monarchical absolutism in these plays did not go far enough for James himself.[10]

A subsequent study, *Power on Display* (1986) by Leonard Tennenhouse, takes a similar position:

> I have borrowed heavily from the beginning of *Discipline and Punish* where Foucault imagines a time before writing was the primary means of social control. He uses a figure – the scene on the scaffold – to represent a culture where power worked more effectively through theatrical display than through writing. In such a culture, with neither police force nor standing army to enforce the law, the representation of punishment was itself an important form of power. Performed in public places, often on raised platforms for all to see, the criminal's torture was carefully designed to be spectacularly horrible, out of all proportion to the crime. Such a scene was supposed to create a visible emblem of the king's absolute authority over the body of the condemned.[11]

Tennenhouse's vision of Elizabethan and Jacobean England is somewhat nightmarish, an absolutist state to which its subjects are so conditioned that its theatre functions as a virtual tool of propaganda. Just as in Goldberg, there is a near total convergence of court, theatre and royal state. The fact that Shakespeare enjoyed royal patronage is generally viewed as the proof that he was unquestioningly complicit with the state ideology. 'The iconography of the stage', he tells us, 'cannot possibly be used against the aristocratic body [...] as if the language of the play [*Macbeth*, in this case] were inherently incapable of speaking against legitimate authority'.[12] I suspect that most readers, viewers and teachers of Shakespeare would baulk at such a statement, because it appears much too crude and one-dimensional to serve as a reading of one of the most nuanced and elusive of playwrights – and the book's reputation since its publication has borne that view out.[13] Unfortunately, this appears to be a step backwards from some of the pre-new-historicist studies I considered in Chapter 2. Both Goldberg's and Tennenhouse's conceptions of Shakespeare's England seem as monological, monolithic and homogenized as Tillyard's. Unsurprisingly, therefore, these studies – as well as Greenblatt's much-discussed essay 'Invisible Bullets' (which was first published in 1981) – proved to be the launching pad for several venomous attacks on new historicism by critics such as Edward Pechter, Richard Levin, Graham Bradshaw and Brian Vickers. All these attacks argued along similar lines: that, far from being a 'new' historicism, it was in fact Tillyard redux; and worse than that, it was anachronistic, unhistorical and flat-out wrong in many of its claims (on which I will elaborate in Chapter 6).[14] How did this happen?

For most of new historicism's critics, the answer is decidedly that it is the influence of Foucault, which as we have seen is strongly evident, especially the late Foucault of *Discipline and Punish*.[15] But surely Foucault's theory of discourse and power relations is marked precisely by its heterogeneity and the refusal to acknowledge a monolithic state for which it has so often been praised. In fact, the conception of power that we find in Goldberg and Tennenhouse appears to be much closer to Louis Althusser's concept of ideology and the ideological state apparatus.[16] Yet Foucault is the much more closely read and frequently cited influence. The 'problem', it seems to me, is not that these early new historicist works have turned back to Althusser, but rather that *analogy* is made to do too much work in their thinking and practice. Foucault's vision of 'panopticism' and the various forms of punishments and tortures he describes in *Discipline and Punish* are seen to be *like* those employed by James I, which are in turn seen to be *like* those depicted in plays by Shakespeare, which are in turn seen to be *emblematic* of the entire Jacobean state. Somewhere in this process, Foucault's ideas about multiple and diffuse power relations go missing. He warns:

> power's conditions of possibility [...] must not be sought in the primary existence of a central point, in a unique source of sovereignty from which secondary and descendent forms would emanate; it is the moving substrate of force relations which, by virtue of their inequality, constantly engender states of power, but the latter are always local and unstable.[17]

For Foucault, the very existence of power relations depends on the fact that society is disparate and made up of what he calls multiple 'sites of resistance':

> Power is everywhere; not because it embraces everything, but because it comes from everywhere [...] Should it be said that one is always 'inside' power, there is no 'escaping' it, there is no about absolute outside where it is concerned, because one is subject to the law in any case? Or that, history being the ruse of reason, power is the ruse of history, always emerging the winner? This would be to misunderstand the strictly relational character of power relationships. Their existence depends on a multiplicity of points of resistance: these play the role of adversary, target, support, or handle in power relations. These points of resistance are present everywhere in the power network. Hence there is no single locus of great Refusal, no soul of revolt, source of all rebellions, or pure law of the revolutionary. Instead there is a plurality of resistances [...] by definition, they can only exist in the strategic field of power relations.[18]

If one thinks about it in very simple terms, Foucault is saying that power exists only where there are multiple parties who are struggling with each other. After all, 'power', in lay terms, is simply the ability to influence and control the behaviour of people. In a classic Foucauldian formulation, however, he seems to assume that, where any two or more parties exist, there will be *de facto* the attempt to exert such influence or control. In this metaphor of the perpetual battle for supremacy we can see flickers of Thomas Hobbes's 'State of Nature',[19] albeit one stripped of its essentialist humanism with individuals – actual people – abstracted out into 'sites of resistance'.

So if all these sites of resistance are so diffuse and in perpetual struggle, how is absolutist hegemony, as envisaged by, say, a Hobbes or a Stalin, even possible? And here Foucault practically rewrites Althusser's 'Contradiction and Overdetermination' in his own words:[20] 'One must suppose that the manifold relationships of force take shape and come into play in the machinery of production, in families, limited groups, and institutions, and the basis for wide-ranging effects of cleavage that run through the social body as a whole'.[21] A similar process accounts for wide-scale change:

> Resistances do not derive from a few heterogeneous principles; but neither are they a lure or a promise that is of necessity betrayed [...] [T]hey [...] are distributed in irregular fashion: the points, knots, or focuses of resistance are spread over time and space at varying densities, at times mobilizing groups or individuals in a definitive way, inflaming certain points of the body, certain moments in life, certain types of behaviour. Are there no great radical ruptures, massive binary divisions, then? Occasionally, yes. But more often one is dealing with mobile and transitory points of resistance, producing cleavages in a society that shift about, fracturing unities and effecting regroupings, furrowing across individuals themselves, cutting them up and remodelling them, marking off irreducible regions in them, in their bodies and minds. [...] [T]he swarm of points of resistance traverses social stratifications and individual unities.[22]

Foucault's 'cleavages' appear to be very close to Althusser's 'overdetermination', and the contradictions roughly equivalent also to the latter's use of the same term. What is very different, however, is that Althusser can only really see scope for change in an epistemic break, something as all-encompassing as a revolution (for example, the Russian Revolution in 1917), whereas Foucault sees constant flux, and struggle even in apparent coherence (hence the evocative term 'cleavages'). He sees little shifts and fragmentary changes in power relations reconstituting behaviour gradually – although I should note that this 'gradually' does not presume progress, it is not necessarily change for the 'better', but just change in a realignment of power relations. Foucault's history is jagged and volatile; it tells no straight-forward story, no smooth narrative.

He seeks also to remove the notion of the individual agent from history and from his account of power relations. If you recall, in the version of history that G. R. Elton told, change was largely accomplished through the deeds of great and visionary individuals such as Thomas Cromwell, who rewrote laws and centralized administrative offices. Foucault explicitly opposes this:

> It is in this sphere of force relations that we must try to analyse the mechanisms of power. In this way we will escape from the system of Law-and-Sovereign which has captivated political thought for such a long time. And if it was true that Machiavelli was among the few – and this no doubt was the scandal of his 'cynicism' – who conceived the power of the Prince in terms of force relationships, perhaps we need to go one step further, do without the persona of the Prince, and decipher power mechanisms on the basis of a strategy that is immanent in force relationships.[23]

This anti-humanist vision of history, which writes out the individual, is inherited by new historicists. Greenblatt, for example, writes in *Renaissance Self-Fashioning* (1980):

> When I first conceived this book several years ago [...] it seemed to me the very hallmark of the Renaissance that

> middle-class and aristocratic males began to feel that they possessed [a] shaping power over their lives, and I saw this power and the freedom it implied as an important element in my own sense of myself. But as my work progressed, I perceived that fashioning oneself and being fashioned by cultural institutions – family, religion, state – were inseparably intertwined [...] Indeed, the human subject itself began to seem remarkably unfree, the ideological product of the relations of power in a particular society.[24]

In this, we can begin to see how the new historicist position of the early-mid 1980s hardened into its orthodox view of Shakespeare's England being a site in which authority and the machinations of power could not be resisted. Although they share this anti-humanist view of the individual as being almost entirely 'unfree', there is a small but crucial difference between the new historicists and Foucault. In new historicist thinking, different discursive fields – let us say, literature, the theatre, the court, the gallows – are marked not by their *difference*, but by the fact that they share a common thread or 'logic'. And this logic is what makes their leaps through analogies – from gallows to court masque, from church sermon to theatre performance – possible. I do not believe that Foucault shares this idea of a cultural logic, which, again, appears closer to Althusser's concept of 'Ideology' (big 'I', as in the official top-down ideology of the state). And so we have the curious scenario in which new historicists in their theoretical writings praise Foucault for his heterogeneous view of power – while distancing themselves from Marxists like Althusser (who insisted on the centrality of the state and its apparatuses) and defining themselves against the monolithic 'spirit of the age' readings made by Tillyard and other critics from the 1940s – while at the same time in their critical practice appearing to replicate the worst tendencies of both Althusser and Tillyard.

I do not think this conundrum can be resolved by looking at these early new historicist works. In the late 1980s and early 1990s, as new historicism started to become more dominant, three major movements took place. The first was that new historicism itself began a process of being anthologized, refined into textbooks, collections of essays, and assimilated at the top of what is essentially the canon of contemporary Shakespeare criticism. The second was that, with the rapidity of its success and assimilation into mainstream scholarship and criticism, new historicism suffered a wave of attacks from traditional scholars from the right, and from cultural materialists and other Marxists from the left, as well as from feminists – all arguing in differing ways that new historicism retained too little scope for agency and subversion because it could not accept any dents in the robust armour of containment. In the third, partly as a result of their ossification into a set of bullet points about power and containment which could then be attacked, new historicists sought more fully to articulate and modulate their positions. Greenblatt did so in his introduction to *Shakespearean Negotiations* (1988) and Montrose both in his essay 'New Historicisms' (1992) and in his introduction to *The Purpose of Playing*. Both shared a discomfort for being identified with constructing 'monolithic entities' in their work.[25]

Greenblatt refines a method and concept he'd been developing throughout the 1980s: cultural poetics, an approach to literature which traces the transference of 'social energy' between disparate and distinct social practices. Here, like Foucault, Greenblatt conceives of culture not as 'a single coherent totalizing system', but as 'fragmentary, [and] conflictual'. It consists of social practices that are 'crossed, torn apart, recombined, set against each other [...] diminished, exalted, evacuated'. And through these constantly undulating practices run various forms of 'social energy': 'Power, charisma, sexual excitement, collective dreams, wonder, desire, anxiety, religious awe, free-floating intensities of experience'.[26] Greenblatt is particularly interested in the moments in which social energy transfers from one mode of social practice to another. Particularly for the purposes of his study he is interested in the transference of energy from, for instance, the pageantry of the royal court or the church sermon to Shakespeare's theatre. He identifies five different types of transference from other contexts to the theatre:

1. Appropriation, that is, of objects and language available to the common currency of the public domain. For example, ordinary words such as 'never'.
2. Purchase, that is, of symbolic objects, such as costumes or props from specialized contexts. For example, a pope's mitre or a royal crown.
3. Acquisition through simulation, that is, of practices already understood to be theatrical. For example, the plays-within-the-plays found in Thomas Kyd's *The Spanish Tragedy* or Shakespeare's *Hamlet*.
4. Metaphorical acquisition, that is, of practices that can only be alluded to because of censorship in order to speak the unspoken. Greenblatt's example is the substitution of 'Jove' for 'God', the latter of which was subject to a £10 fine if uttered on stage.
5. Acquisition through synecdoche or metonymy, that is, of the whole of a given practice through the representation of one part of it. For example, think of the prologue to *Henry V*, 'Into a thousand parts divide one man' (1.1.25), in which the chorus asks the audience to imagine a handful of actors as whole armies.[27]

Greenblatt is particularly fascinated with the moments of what he calls 'negotiation' that occur in these transferences. This is clearly built on top of Foucault's notion of power relations, which I outlined above, but Greenblatt replaces the necessarily conflictual 'sites of resistance' with the much more moderate idea of negotiation and exchange. The moment is more like a frisson, something thrilling and exciting, than an instance of struggle. In this difference between Foucault and Greenblatt, we can see immediately what I was hinting at with the epigraphs at the start of this chapter: Greenblatt's language, as Howard Felperin says, is 'basically mercantile, even strangely monetarist'.[28] In conceiving of a 'social energy', new historicism mirrors the flow of currency in the capitalist free market. In its so doing, we can see once more the self-reflective mirror that haunts the postmodern critic unable to escape him or herself in the attempt to recover the unrecoverable past. And Greenblatt, more than anyone, is acutely aware of this: 'if I wanted to hear the voice of the other, I had to hear my own voice'.[29] Indeed, elsewhere, he views new historicism as being born out of its own historical context: Ronald Reagan's America, Milton Friedman's America[30] – the corporate America at once prophesied and eulogized by Ned Beatty's demonic business magnate, Arthur Jensen, in the 1975 film *Network* in the speech quoted above. In a very real sense, the Renaissance England imagined by Greenblatt is one that might only be imagined by an American. As Harold Veeser put it, in a very lively account, 'literature in capitalism requires a capitalist poetics'.[31]

But this is not to say that Greenblatt necessarily endorses that vision, but rather that his work can be seen as one long attempt fully to come to terms with it, 'not as a unitary demonic principle, but as a complex historical movement in a world without paradisal origins or chiliastic expectations'. 'For capitalism', in Greenblatt's view, 'has characteristically generated neither regimes in which all discourses seem coordinated, nor regimes in which they seem radically isolated or discontinuous, but regimes in which the drive towards differentiation and the drive towards monological organization order simultaneously, or at least oscillate so rapidly as to create the impression of simultaneity'.[32] To put this in very concrete terms: imagine a group of teenagers at a contemporary school, one girl has blue hair and the latest fashionable trainers, and her friends celebrate her for her expression of individuality, soon enough getting their own hair dyed blue and their own fashionable trainers; at the same time, another girl decides not follow the trend and ends up being mocked and bullied for her choice by the others, despite, ironically by this point, being the only girl without blue hair and fashionable trainers. We can recognize at once the contradictory nature of capitalism to which Greenblatt refers: simultaneously appearing to celebrate differentiation while driving towards group conformity. The bullied schoolgirl, of course, does not really represent a subversion of the members of the dominant group – she is not resisting them by refusing to dye her hair blue or wear fancy trainers – but rather, she is confirming them in their own sense of self-identity. In fact, structurally, the bullied schoolgirl exists not to satiate some deep-seated sadism in her peers, but rather as a warning to those who might consider genuine non-conformity to be an option. As David Foster Wallace, rather worryingly, pointed out when talking of a similarly imagined, and similarly bullied, schoolboy:

> When his peers are ostracizing the SNOOTlet or giving him monstrous quadruple Wedgies or holding him down and taking turns spitting on him, there's serious learning going on. Everybody there is learning except the SNOOT – in fact, what the SNOOTlet is being punished for is *precisely* his failure to learn [to speak in the correct idiom of the schoolyard].[33] (emphasis in original)

But at the same time, going back to my group of school girls, we know that, if the original trendsetter next month decides to dye her hair green and start wearing sandals, the chances are that her friends, once again, will follow ... I do hope our other schoolgirl doesn't choose that moment to dye her hair blue or persuade her parents finally to get those trainers! But if we stick with this microcosm, and zoom out a little: our unfortunately bullied girl comes top of most of her classes, and her parents have very good jobs, the teachers like her, and she is never told off by them, she also happens to be the school librarian. Our blue-haired girl comes from a broken home, struggles in class, frequently plays truant, and plans to leave school at the age of sixteen – in fact, she is currently facing possible suspension precisely because of her blue hair. Can we say, easily, who has 'power'? Can we say who is being subversive? Who is being contained? There are very few easy answers, and yet we recognize everyday life in this little scenario, everyday life under capitalism. And there is, I think, a strong flavour of this in Greenblatt's 'cultural poetics'. We can see plainly how he moves beyond the cruder appropriations of Foucault found in Goldberg or Tennenhouse.

Similarly, Montrose is at pains to move beyond the 'hopeless inadequacy of the subversion-containment model'. For Montrose, one of the key issues is that the containment model leaves new historicism open to the charge that it diminishes completely 'the agency of subjects, which it reduces to the illusory and delusive effects of a dominant order'.[34] And he sees this as being partly the result of reductive binary thinking.[35] Instead, he proposes, we need to see the relationship between individuals and their societies as being mutually constitutive and reciprocal. His solution is to expand new historicist reading to bring yet more influences from sociology and anthropology into the theoretical mix. Both in his 1992 essay and later in *The Purpose of Playing*, Montrose turns to the same three quotations taken from Anthony Giddens, Pierre Bourdieu and Mashall Sahlins. Let us take a close look at each of these in turn. From Giddens:

> The structural properties of social systems are both the medium and the outcome of the practices that constitute those systems [...] Rules and resources are drawn upon by actors in the production of interaction, but are thereby also reconstituted through such interaction[.][36]

This, I think, does not amount to much more than saying that rules are redrawn when put to the test in practice. To think of football (soccer in the United States) only one player – the goalkeeper – is allowed to handle the ball. Until 1992, players were allowed to pass the ball back to the goalkeeper who was then able to pick it up. This resulted in some negative tactics, such as time-wasting, especially by teams wishing to protect a slender lead. The 1990 World Cup finals were dogged by such negative tactics, and the authorities responded by introducing the 'pass-back rule', which now prohibited even the goalkeeper from handling the ball if received from a pass by one of his own players. We can see, in Giddens' terms, how the players were interacting with 'rules and resources', and through that interaction thus 'reconstituted' them. This is clear to see in any set of practices that are governed by laws and regulations, but it is more difficult to visualize in cases in which there are no such governing bodies or regulatory systems.

Next, there is the Bourdieu quotation; I must include a little more than Montrose in order to make sense of it:

> The structures constitutive of a particular type of environment (e.g. the material conditions of existence characteristic of a class condition) produce *habitus*, systems of durable, transposable *dispositions*, structured structures predisposed to function as structuring structures, that is, as principles of generation and structuring of practices and representations which can be objectively 'regulated' and 'regular' without in any way being the product of obedience to rules, objectively adapted to their goals without presupposing a consciously aiming at ends or express mastery of the operations necessary to attain them and, being all this, collectively orchestrated without being the product of the orchestrating action of the conductor.[37]

For sure, Bourdieu will not be winning any awards for plain writing any time soon, and *Outline of a Theory of Practice* remains an incredibly dense text. Bourdieu's concept of the *habitus* aims to get precisely at the apparent irreconcilability of our view of ourselves as free agents and the view of individuals as being almost entirely socially conditioned subjects. Each individual experiences his or her own *habitus*, even though also living in a shared *habitus*. Here, we enter some complexity: for Bourdieu, actors are not a direct product of their *habitus*, but rather an interaction between it and their specific set of circumstances and sphere of action (which he calls 'field'). One who enjoys advantages in a given field is said to have 'capital'. And so we come to the following formulation:

[(*habitus*)(capital)] + field = practice

Actors are thus defined by their practices. They gradually change their *habitus* through these practices, even though they are often completely unaware of doing so.

> Each agent, wittingly or unwittingly, willy nilly, is a producer and reproducer of objective meaning. Because his actions and works are the product of a *modus operandi* of which he is not the producer and has no conscious mastery [...] The schemes of thought and expression he has acquired are the basis for the *intentionless invention* of regulated improvisation.[38] (emphasis in original)

We might think of the investment bankers whose actions brought about the financial crisis of 2008: they surely did not know that their packaging of subprime mortgages would bring about the conditions for the near-economic collapse of Greece; and, much like the footballers whose negative tactics brought about the pass-back rule, by their practices they brought about a tightening of financial regulations. But Bourdieu is thinking about change not only on a global scale but also on a more micro, day-to-day level. 'The *habitus* acquired in the family underlies the structuring of school experiences [...] and the *habitus* transformed by schooling, itself diversified, in turn underlies the structuring of all subsequent experiences'.[39] If we think back to my group of hypothetical school girls: we can see that the blue-haired girl's rebellious stance when it comes to her choice of hair dye and footwear might be some consequence of her troubled family background, and, in turn, how the bullied girl's exemplary behaviour in class and good results might be the product of her 'good upbringing'. And the behaviour of both, has an unconscious impact on the future constitution of the *habitus* of each of them. And, in all likelihood, that *habitus* will, in turn, have an impact on how they interact with other social settings throughout their lives.

Finally, Montrose turns to Sahlins:

> History is culturally ordered, differently so in different societies, according to meaningful schemes of things. The converse is also true: cultural schemes are historically ordered, since to a greater or lesser extent the meanings are revalued as they are practically enacted [...] By the 'structure of conjecture' I mean the practical realization of the cultural categories in a specific historical context, as expressed in the interested action of the historical agents.[40]

For Sahlins, social change comes about as the unintended consequence of when social practices, rooted in traditional systems of meaning, are applied in novel circumstances. Sahlins's own example, in *Islands of History*, is the arrival of Captain James Cook at the island of Kauai in 1778. Cook, when he first arrived, was taken by the Hawaiian natives to be one of their gods, Lano, but a year later was murdered by them at Kealakekua Bay. It is a fascinating account of a clash of cultures, each of which does not understand the other. What he notes, however, is that the Europeans and the Hawaiians could not help but assimilate each other in their 'systems of meaning'. Just as one example: for the Hawaiians, a central organizing principle in society was sex and sexual intercourse – and the sexual appetite of the Hawaiian women, and the culture's apparent obsession with sex, seems to have stunned the puritanical Cook and his men. For the Europeans, trade and private property were centrally important. Sahlins documents how, in time, the Hawaiian women and Cook's men joined in sexual union. For the former this held a mythically symbolic and, most importantly, social significance: since Cook was identified with Lano, a woman sleeping with one of his men might enjoy social elevation. However, Cook's men could understand this only in terms of service in exchange for goods – and mistook the women for prostitutes. This arrangement actually transgressed cultural taboos on both sides of the encounter: Hawaiian customs prohibited men and women from eating together (Cook's men fed the women coconuts and bananas), while Cook had forbidden his men from sleeping with any of the women for fear of spreading venereal diseases. So traditional meanings were put at risk by the new systems that were generated by the event of these two groups of people meeting. Hence Sahlins's term, 'structure of conjecture': each culture reacts to the events according to the understanding of their existing cultural categories, and the interaction between these two perceptions produces significant change for both cultures – and in the case of Cook himself it eventually cost him his life.

Let us return to Montrose:

> With such perspectives [i.e. of Giddens, Bourdieu and Sahlins] in mind, we might entertain the following propositions: that the processes of subjectification and structuration are both interdependent and ineluctably historical; that the apparent systematicity of society is perpetually produced, adjusted, and transformed by means of the interactive social practices of individuals and groups; and there is no necessary relationship between the intentions of actions and the outcomes of their actions – in other words, that their effectivity is conjectural or situational and, to varying degrees, contingent.[41]

And so we reach a point in new historicist thinking that is much more complex and nuanced than the simple idea of 'containment'. Individuals are still not exactly autonomous or free, but through their practices, retain a certain degree of agency, even if this agency is more unintended or unwitting than we might typically think it – this agency is not the

Anthony-Robbins-like power to control one's own destiny through willpower, but rather a sort of passive-automatic agency that comes as a by-product of interacting with one's social environment. Later on in the book, Montrose describes an example of this when Shakespeare's company, the Lord Chamberlain's Men, accepted the Earl of Essex's commission to perform *Richard II* at the Globe on 7 February 1601 on the eve of his rebellion against Elizabeth I. Montrose does not think that Shakespeare and his company had any political motivations – that is, they were not willingly endorsing the rebellion, or becoming complicit in the conspiracy. Rather, they 'seem to have been motivated by a combination of social deference [after all, Essex was an *Earl*] and commercial gain. The players' acceptance of the conspirators' commission exemplifies the unstable conjunction of patronage-based and market-based modes of cultural production that was characteristic of the public and professional theatre; it aptly manifests the ambiguous status of the Shakespearean stage within the shifting socio-economic and cognitive frameworks of late Elizabethan England'.[42] The Lord Chamberlain's men were just going about their everyday practice, and yet they might have unwittingly played a role in bringing down the Queen. In a reading such examples as this, we can see Veeser's idea of new historicism as a 'capitalist poetics'.

Montrose puts forward a very interesting theory of history, which radically updates Althusser's idea of subjects working in ideology and reproducing it 'by themselves'. They do work by themselves, but very often the immediate interests of individuals have very little to do with the continued renewal of the ideological state apparatus. In capitalist societies, the immediate interest is often quite obvious: self-betterment through monetary gain and professional or social advancement. Or we might allow some more modest interests: provision for one's family, adequate food and shelter, the stuff of Braudel's *longue durée*. Althusser would argue that all such interests were delusional: this is what individuals must tell themselves in order to carry on doing what they do. As long as workers tell themselves that what they are doing they are doing for their own benefit, and out of choice, they will continue to reproduce the dominant ideology that so ruthlessly exploits them. Amen, so be it. But in Montrose' formulation, in the very process of 'working by themselves' individuals are always-already in some sense engaged in changing their cultures, even if they are totally unaware that this is what they are doing. Change, in a sense then, paradoxically comes about through 'business-as-usual'.

One does wonder, though, how Montrose can account for someone like the Earl of Essex. For G. R. Elton, this was easy: Essex was 'one whose arrogant pride, assurance of high place, hold over Elizabeth's affections, and complete command of popular favour made him a standing danger to the state'. The matter is very straightforward for Elton; Essex's rebellion is the direct result of its leader's personality and his reckless misjudgement of Elizabeth's character, and by the same token its failure is the direct consequence of the hastiness and ineptitude of his planning. In a rather grandiose statement, Elton says, 'the career of Essex is a tragedy in the Shakespearean sense because potential greatness was wrecked by the flaw in the man himself'.[43] It is more difficult to account for Essex's actions from Montrose' formulations. Which structuring principles, interactions with the *habitus*, or structures of conjecture explain why he was rebelling in the first place? Which of them explains why he had the flaw that Elton describes? This is where the influence of structuralism makes itself most keenly felt. Here, we are at the level of Braudel's 'social time': the camera is a little more zoomed-in than it might be for the *longue durée*, but we still cannot recognize individual faces. Even though Essex and even Shakespeare himself are players in this particular historical moment, we view them from afar, and huddled together: they are abstracted from one another as being two groups of agents, each with their demarked fields of practice, 'conspirators' and 'players' respectively – personality does not really come into it. And this is where, I think, Montrose – in probably the most nuanced and well-developed new historicist account available – fails adequately to theorize the individual subject. I say this because it seems to me that had Essex not been a hothead he might not have lost it on 25 February 1601, and yet new historicist analysis cannot seem to admit that. The fault does not lie with Montrose alone, but with any structuralist mode of thought that does not allow or account for the contingency of individual dispositions. It is true that Bourdieu might argue that Essex's own habitus played a role in making him arrogant and entitled, and so, in some sense, conditioned his response to the situation in which he found himself, but this seems rather unsatisfactory: there are courtiers and nobles from the period who cut very different characters – surely some were shy, some were meek, some were frightened and acted mostly out of fear in self-preservation. How can we say that each of these wildly different responses to the situation are equally conditioned by the *habitus*?

Hence, Frank Lentricchia wonders: 'when Greenblatt says, "myself", who exactly is he talking about?'[44] Similarly, a weary Stanley Fish asks of Montrose's 'special consciousness of the conditions within which he lives' [which he calls 'subjectivity']: 'where does it come from?'[45] I do not think these questions can be answered adequately from the theoretical accounts of new historicism that we have available to us, because, while new historicism delights in its own subjectivity, it cannot account for the individual subject except by recourse to his or her situatedness in culture and history. It can explain how power both constrains and enables individuals, it can even explain social change, but it can't explain why a child has a temper tantrum or why the Earl of Essex was arrogant. This last point cannot be easily dismissed given that new historicism is, above all else, a mode of reading *literature*. Shakespeare plays are populated with characters who have distinct traits and personalities that often appear to be the direct causes of their actions. In the way that, for example, Montrose writes, 'individuals' tend to be rather faceless. We do not get a haughty individual, a moody individual, a determined individual, a feckless individual and so on – the individuals do not, on the whole, appear to be very individual. And this is especially curious when we consider how distinctive Shakespeare's most famous characters are.[46]

In this chapter, we have seen how the earliest new historicist works fell foul of an over-simplistic reading of Foucault, which facilitated their notorious 'containment' thesis. This led them too readily to characterize England under Elizabeth I, and then James I, as a despotic and absolutist state. However, we have also seen that Greenblatt and Montrose in particular took pains to distance themselves from the hard version of the containment thesis, and to articulate and theorize more fully their view of culture in history. Their vision of culture is marked by its dynamism: it is constantly shifting and changing, and seeks to account for the complexity of culture and of the lived experience of individuals to culture, which is deemed to be mutually constitutive and reciprocal. However, new historicism seems unable to account for individuals *as* individuals, with traits and characteristics that might have a contingent impact on history, a symptom of the structuralist anthropology and sociology from which much of its thinking derives.

4

New Historicism in Practice: The Case of *Measure for Measure*

To this point, the thrust of this book has been theoretical; in this chapter, through the lens of a single play, I want to gain a sense of new historicism in practice. For this purpose, I have chosen *Measure for Measure*, because few plays have felt the impact of new historicist readings quite as readily. In 1989, when T. F. Wharton claimed '*Measure for Measure* is currently Shakespeare's most popular play',[1] he was almost certainly overstating the point, but the very fact that he felt that a case might be made reveals something of the level of renewed interest in the play. This is not to say that critics before the 1980s had neglected it – indeed as Michael Jamieson pointed out, from 1930 to 1970 'the bulk of criticism on *Measure for Measure* [...] almost rivals that on *Hamlet*'[2] – but rather that a play explicitly concerned with modes of power and justice, which also invites topical readings, represented a perfect and highly visible site on which new historicists could make their mark, and new historicists have been drawn to the play like moths to a flame. With the exception of Louis Montrose, who has focused more on the comedies in general, every major new historicist practitioner has produced a reading of the play. Therefore, by considering these readings – six in total:

those by Jonathan Goldberg, Leonard Tennenhouse, Stephen Greenblatt, Steven Mullaney, Leah S. Marcus and Craig A. Bernthal, chosen for their prominence – we can take in the range of new historicist practice in its many variations.

Long before the advent of new historicism, *Measure for Measure* had been tied to its historical moment by the many critics who saw a parallel between the Duke and James I, who became king in July 1603 at about the time the play is estimated to have been written. The basis for this parallel rests on a number of notable connections between the two figures. The first is that we have a record from the Revels Account that 'On St Stiuens night [26 December] in the [Banqueting] Hall A play Caled Mesur for Mesur', by 'Shaxberd', was performed in 1604.[3] The recently crowned king was almost certainly present. Second, the mix of equitable justice and temperance that the Duke seems to advocate in the play mirrors arguments made by James in *The True Lawe of Free Monarchies* (1598) – and especially in *Basilikon Doron* (1603), which 'was selling like hotcakes in London'.[4] A third similarity is found in the Duke's speech at the start of the play:

> I'll privily away. I love the people,
> But do not like to stage me to their eyes:
> Though it do well, I do not relish well
> Their loud applause and *Aves* vehement;
> Nor do I think the man of safe discretion
> That does affect it. (1.1.67–72)

This is taken to reflect the oft-repeated anecdotal evidence that James did not like crowds, and his preference for ruling in absentia, leaving the day-to-day running of the state to his 'little beagle' Robert Cecil, the Earl of Salisbury.[5] But it also echoes his phrase from *Basilikon Doron*: 'for kings, being public persons by reason of office and authority, are [...] set [...] upon a public stage in the sight of all people, where all beholders' eyes are attentively bent to look and pry in the least circumstance of their secretest drifts'.[6] James advocates that the king should move carefully with 'secret actions'. Since he was dispensing advice to his son, he may have been thinking of his own father, James V of Scotland, who was nicknamed the 'King of Commons' because he was known to have disguised himself as the 'Gudeman of Ballangeich' to move among his subjects incognito.[7] The similarities to the Duke's secret actions in *Measure of Measure* are remarkable.

Using these details Francis Fergusson, writing in 1961, made a reading that perhaps epitomises the 'old' historicist view of this play, which, while its emphases are markedly different, also in interesting ways anticipates new historicist readings:

> A number of critics have disapproved of the Duke, on the ground that his ways are devious, but there are many reasons for thinking that Shakespeare saw him as a model prince. He may have had in mind the half-legendary Haroun al-Rashid, the wise Caliph who wandered among his people in disguise to study their ways. More probably, he was thinking of King James himself, who 'loved the life removed', as the Duke says [...] James explained the duties of the monarch to his son in an epistle called *Basilikon Doron*, in terms which the Duke would have approved: the ruler is responsible not only for the political and economic welfare of his people, but also for their education and spiritual welfare. Duke Vincentio is certainly trying to teach and lead his people through his experiment in government. As stage-director or showman, he is seeking to reveal the truth about human nature and government to the audience in the theater. The Duke (like Prospero in *The Tempest*) is one of Shakespeare's figures based on the analogy between the ruler of the city and the ruler of the theater: each is responsible for the 'truth' in his own way.[8]

For Fergusson, then, the Duke is essentially a benevolent character, who in his disguise as the friar is figuratively as well as literally playing the role of a good 'father' to the people of his city. As we shall see, generally, the new historicist twist on this has been to overturn this view of a benevolent duke and instead see him as working insidiously to reinforce his power and contain subversion. The question becomes less about whether he is working in this way, which is taken as a given, and more about the extent of his success or failure in this aim.

Before getting to those readings, it is worth pointing out that, by the early 1980s, the view outlined by Fergusson had been fiercely disputed. First, even among those who did accept some form of political allegory between James and the Duke, there was no consensus as regards the play's attitude towards its protagonist.[9] Second, the idea that the Duke represents James at all was subjected to serious scrutiny. The most prominent attack came from that latter-day bane of new historicists, Richard Levin, who poured his customary vitriol on earlier historicist studies for their 'occasionalist approach'.[10] Levin mocked the tendency of these critics to produce what he called the 'King James version' of *Measure for Measure*, and ridicules their 'fluellenism' – the term he coined after the Welsh captain found in *Henry V*, who is so intent to push his parallel between the king and Alexander the Great that he seizes on apparent similarities, in fact, isolated and insignificant coincidences, while being blind to obvious differences.[11] Fairly recently, following Levin, Kevin A. Quarmby has found cause to dispute these types of readings also, especially the characterization of an 'anti-social, politically incompetent or reclusive' James, which he argues is based on partisan anti-Stuart 'Whiggish' accounts of his reign that sought to assassinate his character.[12] While acknowledging that there are many similarities, Ivo Kamps and Karen Rabner nevertheless point out 'many striking differences between James and the Duke',[13] including James' anti-Catholicism, preference for early marriage (the Duke is a bachelor) and for social rank (the Duke arranges a marriage between Lucio and a commoner), and the fact that he sees murder as a crime (while the Duke pardons Barnardine). Kamps and Rabner then go on to say that, despite those differences, it's still entirely possible that audiences spotted and responded to the similarities.

For our purposes – that is, in considering new historicist approaches to the play – I am not entirely convinced that it particularly *matters* whether the Duke was or was not intended as a simulacrum for James. If you cast your mind back to Chapter 1, new historicism had already professed to dispense with any desire to find an objective truth (and contested the idea that there ever could be one); history is in their view always-already a construction (which renders the objections in Quarmby's essay virtually redundant). Marcus is even explicit about delighting in the incompatibility of the multiple contexts of texts: 'nexuses of contradiction'.[14] I think to criticise new historicism on the grounds of historical accuracy is, paradoxically, to misread and misunderstand what it is trying to do, which is explicitly (and playfully, mischievously even) to destabilize and expose the clear-headed, evidence-minded, pragmatic 'objectivity' that a critic such as Levin claims to represent. As a proponent of the neo-Aristotelian Chicago school, Levin might be seen as one of several English Lit incarnations of the mindset we saw in G. R. Elton (and I will return to this in Chapter 6). For now, I just want to note that these types of critiques are misplaced, akin to criticising a vegetarian restaurant for not selling enough meat. It is to miss new historicism's own self-consciously postmodern frivolity. To those who maintain some idea of a knowable 'objective' truth this might seem like a dirty move, and in some ways it is, because it removes the epistemological grounds on which knowledge is based and from which such criticisms can be made; but I can see no way round this. To question the historical veracity of the link between James and the Duke in new historicist readings of *Measure for Measure* is to question new historicism's very right to exist. I am taking pains to point this out, because I think it is frequently not grasped – plainly, Quarmby, for example, does not grasp it in the aforementioned essay. Neither did A. D. Nuttall understand it in 1996, when he wrote in a new preface to his seminal *A New Mimesis* (1983), that the 'transition from Theory to New Historicism' represented 'the return of fact', 'historical facts of the grittiest kind'.[15] It comes, I think, from a misunderstanding of the word 'historicism', whereby a lay understanding of the phrase (i.e. a study of contexts that inform our understanding of texts) stands in for what *new* historicism actually represents. This is not to put new historicism beyond critique, obviously, but rather to highlight the ways in which it has been misapprehended in practice, which is a consequence of its own under-theorization coupled with its reduction to the same few trotted-out maxims.[16] These sorts of quibbles are also testament to the fact that, whether or not scholars and critics like it, they cannot dispense with theory by focusing on practice: because disagreement over the specific question of James and the Duke actually boils down to a more general and theoretical disagreement about the ultimate knowability of history, which surely has to take place at that level – much ink might have been spared if it had. With that underlined, we can move on to consider new historicist accounts of the play.

The very first move that Jonathan Goldberg makes in his reading of *Measure for Measure* from 1983 is to shift the historical discussion from the particular to the general. Writing partly with Levin's objections to occasionalist readings of the play in mind, he immediately acknowledges and accepts all the differences between James and the Duke, before dismissing them again as being irrelevant:

> Yet criticism is no doubt correct that *Measure for Measure* has a special relationship to the king. In the pages that follow, that relationship, and with it, Shakespeare's relationship to his culture, are explored through the crucial notion that links theater and culture in James's time: representation. Perhaps one hardly need say more than this, that *Measure for Measure* is a play about substitution, replacement – and thus, re-presentation. In it, the power of the theater bears a royal stamp.[17]

Goldberg is not relying on historical *accuracy* to make his argument, but rather a form of cultural logic which can be traced through both the theatre and the court. One objection that might be raised here is that a concept such as 'representation' is so fundamental and so general that it might reasonably be applied to *anything*. It is surely too diffuse to serve. We find a similar problem in Clifford Geertz, who for all his 'local knowledge' and 'thick description' often ends up drawing conclusions that are so general and basic that they might serve for *any* culture. Witness, for example, his Balinese cock fight, which offers the ground-breaking revelation that victory and defeat are important to the Balinese people.[18] We can return to this tendency in Chapter 6, but it is clear that new historicism, at least as practiced by Goldberg, advances not from historical specificity but from generality, which can appear dangerously close to the 'spirit of the age' arguments of older historicists.

Goldberg focuses on the play's apparently endless doublings, substitutions and tautologies:

> The Duke represents James's Divine Right claims; as a divine – a friar – he claims the right not to be subject to the Duke [...] Nothing and nobody escapes the Duke's grasp. [...] In the play, tautology is the Duke's truth, and with it all's good, all's one, reflecting him, serving his ends. We know that we will never know his ends, that the Duke's motives, unrepresented, can never be known. We see a play of representation in which the rule of doubleness is, from the Duke's perspective, endlessly to his credit, representing multiple mirrors of his powers.[19]

The Duke is James' ideal vision of kingship made manifest on the stage, a stage to which, through his patronage and censorship, he is inextricably linked. Thus, in Goldberg's hands, the Duke comes to represent not only James I but also Shakespeare himself as 'the clearest emblem for the relationship of literature and politics in the Jacobean period'.[20]

Goldberg's reading of the play never quite escapes generating the feeling that it is built on clever verbal sleights-of-hand, but this seems to be something of which it is always conscious. Goldberg delights in the post-structural slipperiness of his own wordplay, and it is not surprising to find that his subsequent career saw him delve deeper into deconstruction.

Prefiguring his own reading of the play, made in 1986, Leonard Tennenhouse, with perhaps characteristic bluntness, tells us: 'If Elizabethan drama had a single strategic intention, it was to forge the structural interdependence of monarch and state'. This is the type of sweeping phrase for which new historicism became notorious. Once again, we find that the Duke's disguise reflects 'the monarch's statecraft'. But under Tennenhouse's gaze the play becomes a sustained argument for the natural government of the divinely ordained ruler: the substitutes, Angelo and Escalus, are shown to be plainly inadequate to the task of administering the law, whether dispensing justice or overseeing marriage 'such a function inheres in the monarch alone'. 'By removing the monarch', he argues, *Measure for Measure* demonstrates 'the power inherent in the patriarchal principle itself as [it] invoke[s] a regressive and magical-mythic – notion of the monarchy [...] an earlier, rarified and magical form of patriarchy as the principle of political order'.[21]

It is a less than satisfying reading of the play, because Tennenhouse neither pauses to consider alternatives nor deals sufficiently with the nuances of the text. What if, for example, the Duke doesn't represent the monarch, but rather God himself? In that scenario, the power he vests in Angelo is akin to the power that God supposedly vested in any monarch; and, of course, Angelo is left wanting. Even if we accept the idea that the Duke represents James, is he as perfect and inscrutable as Tennenhouse argues? He doesn't seem to anticipate Angelo's true nature ('A man of stricture and firm abstinence', 1.3.13), is caught off-guard by Angelo's order to murder Claudio despite his wishes to bed Isabella being granted, seems incapable of gaining any control over the play's one truly inscrutable figure, Barnardine, and finally, in what may be seen as a hypocritical moment, proposes to Isabella himself. And how does Tennenhouse deal with Pompey's down-to-earth realist line, 'If you head and hang all that offend that way but for ten year together, you'll be glad to give out a commission for more heads' (2.1. 205–6)? And the fact that it was the Duke in the first place that gave Angelo 'scope' (1.1.64) to apply the law more strictly, knowing fully well that he would do so? Such questions do not really occur to Tennenhouse, because he is too keen to drive home his conclusion. In *Richard II*, as Bolingbroke approaches, hopelessly outnumbered and materially disadvantaged and faced with a ruthlessly pragmatic enemy, Richard – the king who believes most totally in Divine Right – imagines that an army of angels will fly to his rescue (3.2.58–62). The claim is made to seem absurd, because it is painfully obvious to everyone that no angels are going to come to the rescue. Are we to believe that the same playwright who less than a decade earlier so brutally exposed Richard's belief in Divine Right to the harsh realities of Machiavellian politics was trying to reinforce the belief through that most Machiavellian of rulers, the Duke? It seems unlikely. And Tennenhouse's own reading of *Richard II* is curiously silent on the matter.[22]

With Stephen Greenblatt's reading, in 1988, we come down to earth with a Machiavellian thud. For Greenblatt, the play is less an argument for Divine Right than it is a representation of the ways in which James I used 'the techniques of salutary anxiety' to gain the popular support of his subjects. Here, there are two interrelated principles. The first is fairly straightforward: that elaborate displays of power such as torture, public executions or the age-old practice of sticking body parts on the city gates might arouse anxiety in those who witness such spectacles and so ensure their subordination. But this 'may also go too far', and if punishments are too harsh or indiscriminate the monarch might risk rebellion. And so the second principle is that selective clemency – that is, an act of mercy from the monarch in a situation in which he might not have been so lenient – turns 'anxiety [...] into gratitude'. Greenblatt's example is James' response to the Bye Plot: the first three conspirators, Watson, Clarke and Brooke, were executed; Brooke about a week after the first two and apparently to a stunned silence. But the final three, Grey, Cobham and Markham were assembled on the scaffold only to be reprieved at the last minute, and to much general cheering. 'So too the audience may have cheered the flurry of pardons at the end of *Measure for Measure*'. This is, of course, a nuanced and clever version of Greenblatt's containment thesis: here, power arouses anxiety only to quell it, in exchange for the 'gratitude, obedience, and love' of their subjects. This gives a cogent pretext for several of the Duke's decisions that have long troubled critics: such as why he leads Claudio to believe that he is going to die, and Isabella to believe that he is dead – not to mention why he leaves the law in Angelo's hands in the first place. For this reading to work, we would have to believe that the Duke deliberately engineered the scenario to cast himself in the best possible light at the end of the play with his litany of pardons. But Greenblatt does not see the Duke's power as being perfect, and he walks us through several examples of his failing to shape anxiety in the way that he wants: it does not really work in the case of Juliet, in the case of Claudio, 'the magnificent emblems of indifference [...] the drunken Barnardine and the irrepressible Lucio', or, indeed, 'society at large'. In fact, 'the duke's strategy has not changed the structure of feeling or behaviour in Vienna in the slightest degree'. In the end, all it serves to do is give the audience pleasure, but Shakespeare himself remains committed to salutary anxiety 'as a powerful theatrical technique'.[23] Greenblatt is making two distinct points in this reading: on the one hand, he maintains that salutary anxiety and its subsequent transformation by mercy into gratitude, obedience and love *is* a powerful method of social control for rulers; on the other, he argues that Shakespeare treats the method ironically, and highlights the fact that it is fallible and subject to fail, even though he still favours using it – or at least a representation of it – in his own theatrical practice. Here, we can see Greenblatt making good in practice his own theoretical promise to move beyond the hard version of the containment thesis. He is always alert to the complexities of Shakespeare's text and does not attempt to flatten it to serve his conclusions. At the same time, however, like Goldberg and Tennenhouse, he does detect a certain cultural logic – in this case the principle of anxiety – that Shakespeare's play shares with the moment of its gestation.

In another reading from 1988, like Greenblatt, Steven Mullaney recounts the story featuring Grey, Cobham and Markham, and a second tale, of James hanging a cutpurse who was taken in his retinue while passing through Newark-upon-Trent. For Mullaney, this second event is notable, because Sir John Harrington was worried by the fact that the man had been hanged without a trial. James' 'intrusive display of sovereign authority suggests a monarch who does not recognize the limits of his power or his domain, who might pass judgment as readily on his subjects' thoughts and intention as on their deeds'. Here, the Grey, Cobham and Markham story is seen as another display of power. When he turns to *Measure for Measure*, Mullaney views it as 'a searching exploration of the shape a more intrusive power might take'. Again, he finds it fails utterly in the case of Barnardine, who represents the limits of power. It does work though, for Isabella, who, subjected to the Duke's manipulations, 'gradually relinquishes her sense of self as a fixed and essential entity and begins to view her role as a role, to regard herself as an interchangeable commodity [...] an object of male desire'. Mullaney seems not to believe that Isabella's silence at the Duke's proposal at the end of the play can be taken as resistance, for it is 'too late for resistance', her former image – that of the chaste and innocent novice nun – has already been shattered. 'Her shock at the Duke's proposition is not because it is unimaginable but because, as she realizes at this moment of retrospective clarification, it has become inevitable'. The play with its acute sense of 'being observed – of having been always and already observed' is seen to dismantle, secularize and internalize 'the structures of Christian anxiety, especially the psychological tyranny of pastoral inquiry'.[24] Here, we are firmly back in Foucault's Panopticon, although we might ask why Mullaney seems more interested in cases of its apparent success (Isabella, Angelo) than he is with the surely more interesting and remarkable case of its failure (Barnardine). Of course, we might also ask about whether his reading of Isabella is necessarily warranted: this is a woman who was prepared to let her brother die rather than give up her chastity and who practically disowns him for even daring to ask her to do so (3.1.137–47). She surely went along with the Duke's schemes not because her self-image was shattered but, rather, because, as Cedric Watts points out, she is 'consistent in accepting the authority of a person she knows and trusts as a spiritual adviser':[25] as a novice she would surely heed the guidance of a friar. In her view, would not the Duke represent just another 'proud man, / Dressed in a little brief authority [...] like an angry ape / Play[ing] [...] fantastic tricks before high heaven' (2.2.121–2; 124–5)? It is surely significant that Shakespeare gave that speech to her and not to the Duke. In any case, Mullaney seems too quick assume that her acceptance of the proposal is 'inevitable'.

In yet a third new historicist reading from 1988, Leah S. Marcus focuses on the play's location. Why is it Vienna of all places? And isn't it really just a simulacrum of London? Marcus's style is more overtly archival than any of the accounts we have hitherto witnessed, and her work, while still being assuredly of the 'new' variety, represents a distinctly different type of historicism. This distinction is seldom actually articulated, and Andrew Barnaby and Joan Wry do well to draw our attention to it, in a footnote: 'Although the two types are often related, we might distinguish topical readings from "ideological" readings, those which posit a historically specific meaning for the play in relation not to any particular event in James's reign but to some dominant cultural code'.[26] We have already seen how Goldberg, Tennenhouse, Greenblatt and Mullaney are emphatically examples of the latter. As I mentioned earlier, Marcus takes obvious pleasure in playing with the former type of reading – topical reading – but she does not tie texts to single events but rather to multiple events. In effect, this allows her to have her cake and eat it too – that is, she is at once able to indulge in the sort of old-fashioned E. K. Chambers-like archival historical work that clearly motivates her, while not insisting on the objective 'truth' of any one link between text and event. *Puzzling Shakespeare* (1988) is also perhaps the *example par excellence* of the new historicist commitment to Geertzian 'local knowledge'. Marcus is committed throughout to what she calls 'local reading'. And, in the case of *Measure for Measure*, 'nearly everything depends upon place'.

In her reading of the play, Marcus maps out the London of 1604 with John Stow as a guide, taking care to note its relatively autonomous locales. She then tells of 1604, and the coronation pageant of James I, which 'traversed the streets of London not to admire them, but to take possession of them, display his dominance over them' in a symbolic conquest'. And this, according to Marcus, 'did not necessarily sit well with Londoners', who felt their identity and liberty threatened. In this reading, the Duke's conferring of power to Angelo reflects James' similar appointment of a Lord Mayor to govern London in his stead. But, just as the Duke never really leaves Vienna and hovers over the action, James' presence was always felt in London. Marcus then shifts to discuss laws, which she maintains must be seen at the local level – that is of London – as well as in wider contexts: 'London and its environs were a crazy quilt of different legal jurisdictions, some inextricable from topography, others more global, independent of topographical boundaries'. In other words, Marcus sees no single legal system, but competing legal systems, revealing – in the interests of reading *Measure for Measure* – that 'there *was* no single Renaissance understanding of what constituted valid marriage'. Therefore, if 'Shakespeare's "Vienna" is a jittery and confused place when it comes to questions of sexual morality, Shakespeare's London could be said to suffer from a similar insecurity'. Marcus finds an analogue for Angelo in that London, a certain Chief Justice Popham, known for his precision and suspected of hypocrisy: 'part of the game of topicality in "Vienna" would have been the titillating pleasure of measuring the hypocrisy of Angelo against their own civic authorities'. The Duke himself, of course, finds his analogue once again in James, but Marcus ties this specifically to ecclesiastical licensing. On the question of Isabella's silent response to his marriage proposal, Marcus is more hesitant than Mullaney, and insists that 'we should not automatically discount the possibility' that a rejection – or at least a muted response – might have been impossible to stage in 1604. She then draws an unlikely parallel between Isabella and the recently departed Virgin Queen, Elizabeth: 'the duke's conquest over Isabella can be seen as yet another dramatic marginalization of the mythos of Elizabeth'. In perhaps her most tenuous argument yet, Marcus argues: 'Through Isabella, the dead queen and her cult of virginity and national "intactness" are invaded and dominated by an alternative, Stuart ideology of male dominance and imperial conquest'. One gets the impression that Marcus might take a quizzical look at such a stretched topical reading as a moment of triumph.[27]

And, just at this moment, she turns and reads the play *again*, only this time in a second context, taking Vienna to stand for 'Vienna, or some more generalized depiction of a European city'. Suddenly, the Duke is transformed into the Hapsburg Archduke Albert – once of the Spanish Inquisition – and Isabella taken to be her namesake, his wife. The key occasion for the play in this reading is the Treaty of London of 1604, which concluded the Anglo-Spanish war. Marcus continues to spin out 'other potential localizations', like a topical-reading generator, never privileging any single interpretation and insisting at all times on their co-existence.[28] Marcus's practice truly makes good the new historicist promise of a heterogeneous conception of culture, and there is almost entirely missing the sense of a cultural logic found in the work of her peers. But as the multiple topical contexts unfold revealing yet more topical contexts and as the possible connections become more and more spurious, one does wonder if there is a limit to 'local knowledge'. Marcus refuses to find broad patterns, to generalize, to narrow down, to simplify: her will is always towards the diffuse, the manifold, overlapping structures of increasingly complexity. For her, history is messy, and its joy is in its minute details. And there are moments in *Puzzling Shakespeare* in which one can imagine oneself among the groundlings at the Globe in 1604 – true 'thick description'. It is new historicism at its best: transforming a play such as *Measure for Measure* three or even four times during the course of a single reading.

The final reading that I will consider is that of Craig A. Bernthal, made in 1992. He trots out the story about James pardoning Cobham, Markham and Grey, only this time in much more detail, and with Sir Walter Raleigh's trial, which had taken place beforehand, set to the fore. We can see here the critic-as-storyteller, a well-worn new historicist motif. But where earlier new historicists had found Shakespeare using the Duke to embody and endorse the ideology of James I, Bernthal argues that Londoners were wary of the new Scottish king, who had yet to learn how to 'stage himself to the people's eyes'. In his reading:

> the show trials at the end of *Measure for Measure* could [...] be seen as an unmasking of the way in which political theater is used to create power. By placing trial on stage as a kind of theater, Shakespeare may have enabled his audience to achieve the requisite distance for evaluating trial as a political institution. The effect of such an examination could well have been to demystify James's actions, to display him, in the duke's backstage maneuvring, as less like the Wizard of Oz, and more like an ordinary man, behind the curtains, frantically pulling levers to project a mightier image of himself.[29]

In a penetrating and logical examination of the duke's judgements at the end of the play, Bernthal points out that many of the 'crimes' for which various characters are first condemned and then pardoned were not even crimes. The gap between intention and deed is key: even today, bad intentions are not a crime as long as they do not come to fruition. Angelo cannot be sentenced for killing a man who is not actually dead. Even supposing Claudio was really executed, would it have been a crime to have enforced the law? In this reading, the Duke's decisions are seen to be rather arbitrary. Why did he pardon Barnardine, 'an unrepentant murderer'? Bernthal sees the subversive potential in him: 'audience unwillingness to see Barnardine executed disrupts the theater of execution, for it puts the audience on the side of a criminal who refuses to take the process seriously',[30] thus drawing its attention to James' theatricality.

Bernthal sees, with some justification in my view, that the central concerns of *Measure for Measure* are not legal or political but ethical:

> A duke, who starts out proclaiming his desire to restore law and order, pardons everyone, even a convicted murderer, at the end of the play. The duke forces two (and perhaps three, if we assume that Isabella is not happy with his proposal) unhappy marriages – hardly a way of discouraging fornication. We have the open silences of the pardoned criminals and Isabella, which could indicate anything from acquiescence to resistance to the duke's actions. What we do not get is a hearty thank-you to the duke from all concerned [...] At the end of the play, one can only wonder whether anything of moral value has been accomplished and whether marriage, as comic closure, will lead to the rejuvenation of a society or merely promote further decay.[31]

For both the Duke and James, their actions come at the price of making their theatrics too obvious to the public, which, paradoxically, has the opposite of the desired effect:

it undermines the moral order and, ultimately, authority in the sovereign. Although Bernthal does not say it explicitly, in such a reading, Shakespeare's play becomes a kind of bemused furrowing of the brow at what seem like overly elaborate theatrical power plays; it asks 'to what end?'. Bernthal's approach is more straightforward than that of either Marcus or Greenblatt, but provides another good example of new historicism moving beyond the containment thesis in practice.

New historicist readings such as (and especially) those that I've considered have prefigured and shaped subsequent readings of the play, which are compelled to acknowledge and respond to them.[32] At their best, these readings have been genuinely creative in their use of the available historical materials to produce new angles from which to approach the text. Of the six readings, here, only two – those of Goldberg and Tennenhouse – could reasonably be accused of positing the hard version of the containment thesis. The others find various different ways to complicate or challenge it. Both Greenblatt and Bernthal find that the Duke's machinations, far from working to contain subversion, actually fail. New historicism's great strength was always in its inventiveness in generating multiple new ways to read plays that had already been read over and over again, and this is given its fullest demonstration in Marcus's *tour de force* reading(s) of the play, which, if nothing else, shows transformative power of context. However, ironically, almost all of these new historicist studies of *Measure for Measure* are made in the same political register. Even Marcus can only seem to imagine contexts that speak to questions of power and the administering of the law. One might argue that this is simply because *Measure for Measure* is a play that is *about* power, centred as it is on the shadowy dealings of a cunning ruler who seems to be conducting a form of social experiment on the people of the city of Vienna. But there are many dimensions to this play – of interest to earlier critics and to current lay audiences alike – that are seemingly untouched by new historicist consideration.

In the first half of the twentieth century, many scholars of a formalist bent were fixated on the problem of categorizing *Measure for Measure* in terms of its genre: it is, of course, along with *All's Well that Ends Well* and *Troilus and Cressida*, one of the so-called problem plays. Perhaps understandably, new historicists appear to show little to no interest in this question. However, it is not the only question on which they show little interest. If I were to outline the most important issues at stake in this play, perhaps for a student seminar discussion, they might look something like this:

1. Why does the Duke abdicate his responsibility to Angelo only to spy on him and the rest of his subjects? What does he hope to achieve? Does he achieve it?
2. What does the Duke represent? What was Shakespeare trying to say through the figure of the Duke?
3. To what extent are the decisions of the Duke in the final trial justified? Is justice really served? Is justice fundamentally incompatible with the Christian concept of mercy? How can Angelo be allowed to 'get away with it'?
4. How does the play view its ostensible heroine, Isabella? How does the audience react to her refusal to give up her chastity in order to save Claudio's life? How about her willingness to go along with the Duke's plan in the 'bed-trick' involving Mariana? And, finally, how do we interpret her silence in response to the Duke's proposal at the end of the play?
5. Why are the characters of Pompey, Barnardine and Lucio in the play? Do they serve to reinforce or undermine the way in which we view the Duke?
6. What is the play's attitude towards sex? Why are the characters all seemingly so obsessed by it? Are Angelo and Isabella sadomasochists?

7 What sense of morality, if indeed any, does the play posit?
8 What are we to make of the mediations on death in the exchanges between Claudio and the Duke?

As we have seen, new historicists have been overwhelmingly concerned with the first three of these issues. On the whole, a strong focus on the Duke and questions of political power have come at the expense of attention's being paid to Isabella, who animated and divided earlier critics, or to questions of moral agency – indeed in Mullaney's reading Isabella's agency is shattered by her interpellation into the Duke's schemes. They have also tended to leave the play's vexed questions about sex and sexuality to feminists and psychoanalytical critics. And, Bernthal aside, they have been virtually silent on *Measure for Measure*'s ethical dilemmas – much to the chagrin of Brian Vickers, who could not resist taking a potshot in his 'General Editor's Preface' at George Geckle's survey of the play's critical tradition, which he used as another opportunity to grandstand his disapproval of recent critical trends:

> The New Historicists Tennenhouse and Mullaney, in the wake of Foucault, effectively reduce the play to an allegory of power, desire, and anxiety, so giving 'the demons of abstraction' free reign [...] The manifestos of both Historicists and Materialists sound grand, but in practice they fail to register the play's real focus, which is ethical. Angelo's desire for Isabella is an instance of natural sexuality, all the more powerful for a lifetime's repression, but he perverts both the state's concept of justice and private human relations by misusing his power over Claudio's life to satisfy his appetite. Like Lucio's treatment of his whore, Angelo instrumentalizes his desire, exploiting Isabella, treating her – in Kant's terms – as a means to an end, not as an end in herself. This fundamental violation of male-female relations is not registered by Historicist

or Materialist approaches, which are essentially amoral, concerned with abstractions and intellectual equations.[33]

While Vickers is perhaps too forceful in insisting that the 'real focus' of the play is ethical (surely we can entertain the notion of multiple and even competing focuses), it is fair to say that new historicists, at least on the evidence of the readings covered in this chapter, have collapsed the moral, and indeed religious aspects of the play, into the political. I do not think this is because new historicism is 'amoral', as Vickers suggests, but rather that it is a symptom of its commitment to the idea of cultural logics. While new historicists maintain that culture is heterogeneous and in constant flux, as we saw in Chapter 3, there is still a notion that certain 'energies' can be traced through its many disparate fields of operation – in Goldberg's reading 'representation', in Tennenhouse's 'patriarchy', in Greenblatt's 'anxiety', in Mullaney's 'pastoral inquiry', and so on. And while these logics are not binding and do not *necessarily* serve a monolithic state, they do serve to make the various different fields – let us say, the political, the theatrical, the religious, the legal, the ethical – less distinctive because they share these common features. In effect, then, it is not only the ethical that is collapsed into the political, but also the theatrical, the religious, the legal and so on. For the new historicists, we do indeed live in a political world. In Chapter 6 we will return to the possible consequences of this aspect of new historicist thinking. For now, it is enough to say that a full account of the play cannot rest on the Duke. It is noticeable that critics have no choice but to return to the same few anecdotes (about James I's political views and writings, his dramatic pardoning of Cobham, Markham and Grey, contemporary uncertainty about the new king and so on) in crafting their readings centred on the Duke; but this is surely to reduce the play's complexities to a set of narrow concerns that it demonstrably exceeds. For example, generations of critics have found Isabella's piety cold, inhumane and narcissistic, especially in her fierce reaction to Claudio's pathetic and desperate pleas to her (in 3.1) to save his life.

But aren't such reactions to the character anachronistic and a failure to understand the novice nun in her context? One might imagine that such a question would be fertile ground for new historicists to plough, an ideal opportunity for 'thick description', but seemingly not. And again the question is left for feminists and traditional scholars to take up.

In this chapter, through the prism of reading *Measure for Measure* and putting under the microscope six new historicist approaches to the play (one from 1983, one from 1986, three from 1988 and one from 1992), we have seen how new historicists in practice make good many of their theoretical promises, including moving well beyond the containment thesis. But we have also seen some of the limitations of new historicism: its apparent inability to give a full account of a play beyond its political concerns and contexts. In the chapters that follow, we will see new historicists attacked again and again for not reflecting on certain issues: by feminists for their silence on gender and general focus on males in positions of power (as we've seen in *Measure for Measure*, the Duke gets the lion's share of the attention at the expense of Isabella); by traditional scholars for their methodological anarchy and collapsing of text into context (and context into text); by the right for their advocacy of postmodern theory; by cultural materialists and the left for their neglect of class issues and tendency to see the state winning out (the latter has not been particularly in evidence here). It is worth stating again, then, in order to keep it in mind throughout these attacks, that new historicism – despite its shortcomings – has produced strikingly original and virtuoso readings of Shakespeare's plays. While George Geckle could no doubt point to historical precedents from earlier critics for virtually all the critical positions put forward by Goldberg, Tennenhouse, Greenblatt, Mullaney, Marcus and Bernthal, he could not claim that any of those earlier critics would have made some of the bold, theoretically informed, and to some eyes even illogical or at least wilfully counter-intuitive, moves that we have witnessed these new historicists make during the course of this chapter.

5

New Historicism and Feminism

So we grew together,
Like to a double cherry, seeming parted,
But yet an union in partition

A MIDSUMMER NIGHT'S DREAM, 3.2.208–10

The rise of feminism in Shakespeare studies mirrors that of new historicism, emerging in the late 1970s and early 1980s, although their geneses are distinct. It is not possible to generalize about the relationship between new historicism and feminism, because 'feminism' *per se* does not represent an approach to literary texts; it is not a methodology, but a political commitment and focus of interest. Therefore, new historicist methods might be appropriated by feminist critics, and to a large extent this has happened. In 1991, Jean E. Howard asked 'whose interests are served by continuing to frame the question of feminism's relationship to "historicism" in agnostic terms?'[1] By 1995, David Bevington could write of an 'uneasy alliance' between feminism and new historicism.[2] Of course, Howard's question presupposes some level of agnosticism and even antagonism towards new historicism on the part of feminists. In this chapter, I hope to trace how new historicism and feminism 'grew together' from their initial sometimes fierce antagonism in the mid- to late 1980s to their eventual union, or at least tacit alliance less than a decade later.

To grasp how feminists have related to new historicism, therefore, it is first necessary to draw a dividing line between so-called first-generation feminist Shakespeareans – whose number we might group, loosely, as including Carol Thomas Neely, Gayle Greene, Marilyn French, Linda Bamber, Lynda Boose, Coppélia Kahn, Janet Adelman and Meredith Anne Skura – and a second group of materialist feminist critics, such as Linda Woodbridge, Karen Newman, Kathleen McLuskie, Lisa Jardine, Dympna Callaghan, Jean Howard, Phyllis Rackin, Valerie Traub, Catherine Belsey and Peter Erickson. Although not true of all those named, for the most part members of the first group were strongly influenced by psychoanalysis – Adelman, Kahn and Skura, in particular, who together with Harry Berger, Jr, arguably represent the most brilliant of the psychoanalytical critics of the 1980s and 1990s. The second group advanced many of their studies by critiquing the assumptions of the first group, which were found to rely on what McLuskie called a 'mimetic, essentialist model' of reading Shakespeare's plays.[3] This complicates the relationship with new historicism, because, from a certain vantage point, the second grouping is allied with new historicism and co-opts many of its tools in making its critiques of the first group. But this view is complicated again by the fact that both groups, at different times, have been critical of new historicism. The latter group, in general, owing both to their political orientation and commitment to a materialist methodology, has found more in common with the more radical agenda of British cultural materialists such as Jonathan Dollimore and Alan Sinfield.

This picture is complicated at yet another level: in the context of battling against attacks from more traditional voices in the academy (such as those of Richard Levin, Graham Bradshaw and Brian Vickers), *all* these various groupings – the new historicists, the first-generation feminists, the materialist feminists, and the cultural materialists – are allied against conventional liberal humanist criticism. This is strikingly demonstrated by the infamous letter sent to the PMLA forum in 1989 protesting the publication of Levin's even more notorious broadside at feminist scholarship, 'Feminist Theatrics and Shakespearean Tragedy'. It was signed by no fewer than twenty-four critics, whose names include representatives from both the groups of feminists identified above: first-generation (Adelman, Boose, Kahn, Neely) and materialist (Belsey, Erickson, Jardine, McLuskie).[4] As we have seen, and will see again in Chapter 6, on other occasions Levin tussled with both new historicists and cultural materialists. So despite their various differences and disagreements, when faced with a figure such as Levin, all four groups unite against a common enemy. And thus we see different levels of allegiance depending on the battle being fought (see Figure 5.1 below).

The clash between the first-generation feminists and new historicists might be seen as a natural consequence of the apparent incompatibility of psychoanalysis, which must at some level maintain a concept of an inherent or natural self, with historicism, which – at least in the variant we have seen

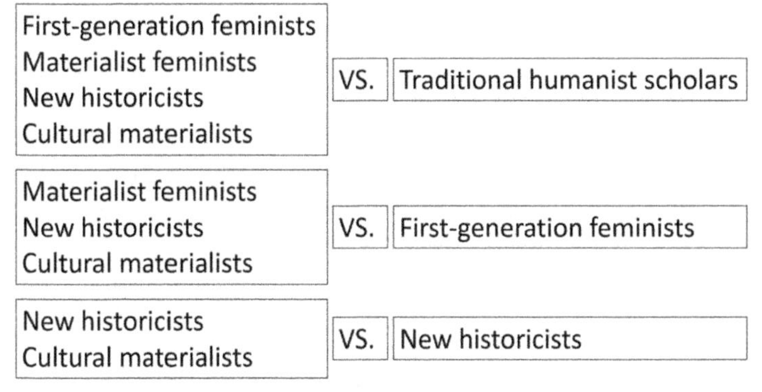

Figure 5.1 *Allegiances of various critical groups in different battles.*

thus far – sees the self as being primarily the product of its social environs. Stephen Greenblatt, for example, accused psychoanalysis of the 'attempted universalization [...] [of] a fixed value of identity [...] a totalizing comprehension, a harmonious vision of the whole' [...] 'achieved [...] only by repressing history, or more accurately, by repressing *histories* – multiple, complex, refractory stories'. For Greenblatt, psychoanalysis represents a form of anachronism when it comes to reading early modern texts. In works by Shakespeare and other dramatists of his period, 'identity is conceived in a way that renders psychoanalytical interpretations marginal or belated [...] psychoanalysis can only redeem its belatedness when it historicizes its own procedures'.[5] This statement goes to the very heart of new historicist belief: Greenblatt cannot entertain the possibility that human beings from Shakespeare's time shared a common psyche with their modern counterparts. Individual identity is seen to be so completely bound up with one's historical and cultural moment that it actually shapes how the mind works.[6]

However, reading reflections from first-generation feminists in various debates, one gains a real sense of them as a group of women living and working in the real world, whose concerns are not theoretical and not about the ultimate causes of the human psyche, but rather about the plight of women in the academy and beyond. They are feminists primarily in the political sense of wanting equality of pay, fair treatment, and so on – which is not to accuse their opponents in these debates of not wanting those things also, but rather to highlight that for the feminists it is *this* concern that comes before all others (theoretical, methodological, historical, etc.). Consider, for example, Gayle Greene's candid response to Levin, which is so firmly rooted in that concern. It will be necessary to quote her at length to demonstrate this:

> From where I sit as a feminist it does not look to me as if I control *PMLA* or much of anything else in the profession. In the late seventies when I and my co-editors were asked

> to submit names of readers for our anthology *The Women's Part: Feminist Criticism of Shakespeare*,[7] we had difficulty coming up with the names of two senior Shakespeareans who would not trash the idea of a feminist reading of Shakespeare; what we encountered again and again was the response I have described – that we were desecrating something sacred [...] When by the early 1980s our book was published and we'd achieved some recognition and were working together – we had become a 'mafia'. I was interested to hear the term 'the black mafia' was applied to a comparable group of revisionist critics in Afro-American studies. I also heard that MLA letter signed by twenty-four feminists referred to as a 'gang-bang'.[8]

By personalizing things to this extent, Greene is breaking some unspoken rules of intellectual conduct. We are given a glimpse into the off-the-record world of whispers at conferences, off-handed comments, fretful discussions between colleagues that would usually go on 'behind the scenes', hidden by the polite façade of the academy. Greene, no doubt, knows what she is doing: exposing what she sees as a professional climate that is hostile to feminism and hides behind the objectivity and 'rules' of the accepted standards of logical debate that the neo-Aristotelian Levin holds so dear. By demystifying the workings of the academy, Greene can show its uglier side. In a seminal essay, her contemporary, Lynda Boose, uses a similar strategy:

> The North American pioneers in this field [i.e. of first-generation feminists] include scholars like Janet Adelman, Shirley Garner (who had previously published under the name 'S. N. Garner', thus doing what I, too, was advised in graduate school to do), Gayle Greene, Coppélia Kahn, Carol Thomas Neely, Marianne Novy, Clara Claiborne Park, Phyllis Rackin, Meredith Skura, Madelon Sprengnether [Gohlke], Carolyn Swift [Lenz], and Linda Woodbridge [Fitz] [...] In surveying the atmosphere of the present

> moment, it seems accurate to say that feminist scholarship right now stands at a crossroads that is as much political as intellectual. In terms of the outward marks of political achievement, what initially began as a feminist inquiry spearheaded by a group of scholars (most out of academic jobs at the time) worked within a mere twelve years to effect substantial changes in the shape and classroom content of American English Departments.[9]

Again, Boose breaks some unspoken rules of convention here: she draws attention to several personal details which call any pretence to scholarly objectivity or ivory-tower authority – which a name like 'S. N. Garner' might conjure – into question. She also draws attention to the marital status of several of her colleagues. She mentions the fact that some of them did not have academic jobs when their earlier work was produced. This is a breaking of the fourth wall of scholarship: it is impossible to read Boose without thinking of these academics as real people operating in a real world. Both Greene and Boose are deliberately drawing attention to the fact that appeal to scholarly objectivity is a luxury that male critics can enjoy, and which can be used as a weapon against their female counterparts.

Back to Greene:

> Older colleagues don't read us; most simply ignore us, hoping that if they wait us out we'll eventually go away. Our contemporaries and younger colleagues, eager to make a space for themselves, either ignore us, writing as though feminist criticism had never happened, or attempt to climb to the top on our bodies, having exposed us as theoretically 'soft,' anachronistic, vulgarly empiricist, naively Anglo-American – whatever: the factions that split feminist scholarship at the moment are not encouraging.[10]

Once more, this is drawing attention to something that for the most part goes unsaid in the academic world: older colleagues are not especially prone to reading the work of their younger counterparts. Realistically, why would they? Once the rank of 'full professor' is reached, they've already climbed the ladder and 'made it'. This certainly seems to be true of the older Shakespeareans still active in the last twenty years of the twentieth century – G. K. Hunter, Phillip Edwards, Frank Kermode, Kenneth Muir to name a few. Most of them resolutely ignored (or else dismissed out of hand with minimal discussion) not only feminism but also new historicism, cultural materialism, deconstruction and the other developments of the 1970s and 1980s. The reality is that when someone has attained the status implied by a job title such as 'King Alfred Professor of English Literature' they have already made their mark in the field – why bother to sully their hands fighting with the young Turks? Levin represented an exception, in deigning to tangle with the younger generation; as Greene said in an aside to Ivo Kamps at a conference, '*at least* Levin reads us'[11] (emphasis in original).It is not clear, here, whether Greene is suggesting that first-generation feminist work was ignored by the old generation because it was carried out by women, or whether she is making the more general point. What is clear, and resoundingly so, is that she and her feminist colleagues felt marginalized, and pilloried from all sides.

This does not come from paranoia, however, but from a genuine concern that feminist issues are occluded:

> A look at the space given to feminist criticism in revisionary anthologies on the Renaissance shows a similar process of erasure: a 1985 anthology has one essay on feminist criticism of Shakespeare, which attacks American feminism for being reductive and essentialist (McLuskie, 'The Patriarchal Bard') a 1986 collection has no 'feminist essays and two gender-related essays[12] [...] Feminist criticism has been absorbed, assimilated, usurped, by new historicists' discussions of politics, power, colonialism, the court, class, ideology – all of which have bearing on gender but, more often than not, are not brought to bear on gender. Is it a

> coincidence that this is the time that *PMLA* – the most prestigious and regarded by many as the best journal in our profession – just happens to publish [Levin's] attack on feminist criticism? It is not my paranoia to imagine that a feminist essay would have been subjected to far more rigorous scrutiny as to the theoretical implications of its positions, would have been required to inform itself more carefully about whatever position it was critiquing.[13]

In short, Greene worries about feminism's being shut up and shut out by scholarship, and that this might include work carried out by new historicists and materialist feminists. If the charge from McLuskie, Howard and others was that these feminists were not historical enough, the counter-claim was that the materialist feminists were not feminist enough.

Boose argues along similar lines, and, in classic first-generation feminist fashion, roots her point more stunningly in the real-world than any made by new historicists, whose style – while sometimes anecdotal and even personal – always maintained, at least in tone, a coolly detached, always-already post-ironic academic distance.

> In the chain of MLA sessions it generated, equal numbers of newcomers and equal distributions of male and female scholars were scrupulously invited [...] the emphasis was on collaboration rather than single voice authority. It seems accurate to say that the work on family construction was itself born inside an atmosphere which was, in psychoanalytic terms, distinctly nurturing, distinctly maternal [...] What feminist scholars did *not* want to happen, however, is exactly what there is by now reason to fear is subtly happening: that the putative 'microcosm' of marriage, family and gender relations, having once been brought into the center of scholarship and made equal with the supposed 'macrocosm' subjects, be tacitly turned into an academic ghetto, a 'little world of woman' where feminist issues could be progressively contained and re-marginalized while

> male scholarship returned under the name of new methodologies to its old study of power and court politics and effectively reconstructed a 1980s version of the Elizabethan World Picture that Renaissance scholars had, but a few years earlier, set out to deconstruct.[14]

For Boose, new historicism's central concern with power itself reflects a bid for power and centrality within Shakespeare studies, which marginalizes other concerns, specifically feminist concerns. If we cast our minds back to Chapter 4, we see that, in the case of *Measure for Measure*, Isabella – central in earlier studies of the play – was necessarily pushed to the margins in new historicist readings that focused squarely on the Duke. For a first-generation-feminist such as Boose, gender matters in every respect: the gender of the critic, the gender of the characters in focus, and the question of whether or not gender is on the agenda. And so she would naturally have reservations about the idea of a privileged male critic writing about a privileged male character (in a play written by the most canonical male author) at the expense of female critics and female characters (and female authors). Once again, the marginalization she perceives is not only theoretical – in print – but embodied in the actual organization of a conference of Shakespeareans. Her account of one annual meeting is revealing:

> Such a mico-macro segregation and such a return to old, gender-based asymmetries of power was, however, what was proleptically dramatized before the audience of the 1982 Shakespeare Association in Boston. On one side of the steel curtain that separated the convention's central and simultaneous seminars, several of the major feminist psychoanalytic critics had been invited to confess their shortcomings in a forum entitled 'The Limitations of Psychoanalytic Criticism.' On the other side of the barrier – where several of the major new historicist critics held forth in an authorative show called 'The Implications of

> The New Historicism' – Coppélia Kahn, speaking from her anomalous position on the second panel, pointed out the disturbing division that the seminar organization seemed to dramatize. In doing so, Kahn seems to have been the first to comment publicly on the incipient schism and the first to call for a consciousness that might prevent it.[15]

In Boose's reading, not only does new historicism send the feminists quite literally next door, it also elides feminist concerns with those of state and power. After directly critiquing Greenblatt's essay, 'Fiction and Friction', in which 'gender disappears' in an all-male discourse, she continues the attack on new historicism more generally:

> Not only the issue of women tends to disappear in new historicism; what also gets erased is the terrain of the domestic microcosm. When new historicism locates itself upon the site of family, sex, and marriage, the literal arena of domestic space has a way of losing its local habitation through its name and turning into its descriptive other. In critical practice that comes perilously close to duplicating the Renaissance political strategies it anatomizes, historicist criticism has of late taken up the 'family' as a topic, only to then redefine it as the locus upon which the political state built *its* power through strategic appropriation, marginalization, and transformation of the family into an instrument of state authority [...] Once again, gender is erased, women are erased, and the historicist critic is busily back at work reconstructing and reproducing an academic microcosm of the absolutist court and its strategies of male power.[16]

This is a clever, if dark twist on the idea, which I discussed in Chapter 1, that new historicists see their own concerns reflected back to them. Boose continues at some length: attacking Jonathan Goldberg (or rather, defending Linda Bamber, his 'whipping girl', from attack[17]), and accusing new historicism of being politically interested in reproducing the very 'institutional forms of absolute male power' with which it is preoccupied.[18]

A year later, in 1988, a year in which the Shakespeare Association of America hosted a seminar called 'Feminism vs. New Historicism', Boose's message found impassioned support from her old sister-ally Carol Thomas Neely:

> A small, interlocked, committed, and first-rate group of critics and the ideology which they promulgate are in the process of coming to dominate the institution of the Renaissance in this country: the conference programs, the journals, the glutted anthology market, and the spare job market, especially the upper level jobs which have generated a game of Renaissance musical chairs in the last several years [...] In spite of all that the new theoretical discourses seem to have in common with feminist criticism, in spite of their appropriation of some of its claims, their effect – not necessarily a deliberate or inevitable one – has been to oppress women, repress sexuality, and subordinate gender issues. All of the topoi of the new approaches: the historicity and intertextuality of texts; the constriction of history to power, politics, and ideology; the denial of unity, autonomy, and identity in authors, subjects, texts; the displacement of women to woman to sexual difference to textuality; the view of man/woman as just one more in an outmoded, interchangeable parade of binary oppositions, have the effect of putting woman in her customary place, of re-producing patriarchy – the same old master plot. In it, women continue to be marginalized, erased, displaced, allegorized, and their language and silence continue to serve the newly dominant ideology. The approaches are not new enough [...] New historicism's insistence on the textuality of history and the intertextuality of literature and other texts has brought into the discourse a wide range of fascinating period texts, brilliantly explicated. But these texts, more often than not, are much like or even identical

> with those favoured by old historical critics. They are male, upper class, hierarchical, prescriptive, virtually literary.[19]

In the view of first-generation feminists such as Boose and Neely, there seems to be a one-to-one correlation between critical and real-life concerns: a criticism that focuses on the way an early modern playwright effaces the agency of women *actually* effaces the agency of women, and, by the same token, a criticism that focuses on finding agency for women (e.g. in Shakespeare's plays) *actually* posits agency for women. And since new historicists, by their own admission, cannot lay claim to any neutral site of objective, disinterested academic analysis, they are 'idealist' critics as much as feminists are. Neely is critical of several other critics for effectively ignoring women in plays – not only Greenblatt, for making Cordelia 'virtually disappear' in *King Lear*, but also Jonathan Dollimore, a cultural materialist, for failing to speak up for the 'silenced' prostitutes of *Measure for Measure* and the materialist feminist McLuskie for doing little else but point out their exclusion.[20] Neely argues that feminists must 'over-read men's canonical texts with women's uncanonical ones' to produce studies that can register 'women's unruliness'.[21] It seems to me that – strange as it may appear – in their focus on the absence of individual agency (for women) in new historicism, cultural materialism and their theoretical progenitors (particularly Michel Foucault and Louis Althusser), Greene, Boose and Neely actually make many of the same points as the liberal humanists we will encounter in Chapter 6. This is 'strange', because, of course, many of those same liberal humanists – Levin, Vickers and so on – were their bitter enemies. Other than the strong emphasis on women in the former case, the critiques of new historicism we get from the first-generation feminists and the liberal humanists are, in fact, virtually identical in terms of their theoretical complaints. We will return to them in Chapter 6.

As should now be clear, first-generation feminist attacks on new historicism by prominent scholars such as Greene,

Boose and Neely took on a confrontational, personalized and oppositional tone. Howard's 'agnostic terms', which I quoted in the first paragraph, reads as quite an understatement. An uncharitable reading of Greene, Boose and Neely might suggest that the real cause of their opprobrium was an anxiety about critical trends passing them by in real time – less about feminism being marginalized, more about their particular brand of it becoming outmoded. I would not necessarily endorse such a reading. Because Greene, Boose and Neely were all committed to a feminist practice that looked for strong women and female agency in literature, in history and in the family, it is entirely understandable that they might be to some degree distraught to find that vision of feminism overturned for one that appeared systematically to deny women agency at every turn and reduced to pointing this out while marvelling at the ingeniousness of patriarchal forms of power. There is no reason to assume any bad faith on their part, even if, with the benefit of almost thirty years of hindsight, we can see that the times – or at least the fickle winds of critical fashion – *were* passing them by. In short, they had fallen out of fashion. This is palpable in Peter Erickson's introduction to *Rewriting Shakespeare, Rewriting Ourselves* (1991), in which he is very plainly, almost nakedly, attempting to transition himself from the sort of psychoanalytically informed feminism that characterized the first generation to a practice informed by new historicism and cultural materialism:

> My first book was written largely within the tradition of American feminist psychoanalytic criticism of Shakespeare as it existed at the end of the 1970s. The development of which this book is a record can be summarized as a shift away from psychoanalytic criticism toward an intensive engagement with new historicism and cultural materialism for the purpose of strengthening feminist criticism by expanding its bases [...] It is too early to speak of a second wave of feminist criticism of Shakespeare, but the first

> wave, having made its contribution, has lost much of its momentum as a sharply defined entity. The original core group of feminist Shakespeare critics has to some extent dispersed; other critics who do not belong to this group and do not share its purview have decisively entered the field. The result is that disagreements within the original group no longer set and control the agenda.[22]

With statements like this, one can see why members of that core group of first-generation feminists were under the impression that they were being shunted to one side. And Erickson's book is a sustained attempt to recruit methods from new historicism and cultural materialism to serve a feminist aim. It can be seen as a sign of its times.

Those times were signalled much more emblematically in the same year as Erickson's study in a volume edited by Valerie Wayne, *The Matter of Difference: Materialist Feminist Criticism of Shakespeare* (1991). One might say that this book is to materialist feminists what, in 1985, *Political Shakespeare* was to cultural materialists: at once a manifesto of sorts, and a litmus-test-collection of the variety of materialist feminist criticism that was on offer in 1991. In her level-headed introduction, Wayne claims that the general approach 'disclaims the universality associated with formalist discourse', while conveying 'a critique of new historicism for its apolitical or recuperative effects and of feminism for its tendencies to idealize or essentialize women'. While she rebukes new historicism for its 'preoccupation with the elite in Renaissance texts' and its tendency to negate the scope for subversion, Wayne also calls time on the first-generation feminists: 'Although I applaud the success of those earlier efforts, critical theory and psychoanalytic theory are at a different point in their development and to call for an extension of those earlier approaches is to ignore the productive complexity of this particular moment'.[23] In other words, the scene had moved on from *The Woman's Part*.

In truth, this did not happen overnight. By 1991, the materialist feminist approach was a strong current in the study of early modern literature that had taken place throughout the 1980s, running parallel to both new historicism and the work of the first-generation feminists. I would include in the publication history: Lisa Jardine's, *Still Harping on Daughters* (1983),[24] which Coppélia Kahn categorized as a book of '"cultural poetics" or "new historicism"' and took 'as a slap on the wrist to feminist critics';[25] Linda Woodbridge's *Women and the English Renaissance* (1984), a scholarly affair that is not much concerned with questions of theory or the current debates around it but which arguably does a more thorough job of investigating misogyny and representations of women on the early modern stage than does Jardine's book; Catherine Belsey's *The Subject of Tragedy* (1985), which, while less theoretically inflected than her later work, still represents a sustained attack on liberal humanist criticism from a feminist and Marxist perspective; Dympna Callaghan's *Women and Gender in Renaissance Tragedy* (1989), which builds in various ways on the studies by Jardine, Woodbridge and Belsey;[26] Karen Newman's *Fashioning Femininity and English Renaissance Drama* (1991), which riffs on the title of Greenblatt's *Renaissance Self-fashioning*, and undoubtedly succeeds in its aim of overturning 'the critical lament of the victim characteristic of some feminist work' (she cites the Boose essay I have discussed in this chapter as a good example of this) and 'the new historicist's resigned claims of "containment" as well'.[27]

While it is not true of every materialist feminist work produced during this period, I think it is generally fair to say that the majority of these studies are united in borrowing key tenets from Marxist theory, especially Louis Althusser's concept of interpellation and insistence that ideology has a material existence, which are both frequently cited. Although the emphases are more squarely on gender, and, in particular, on the representation of women and the question of misogyny than is the case in the work of Alan Sinfield or Jonathan Dollimore, methodologically and theoretically there is not much to distinguish the materialist feminists from cultural materialists, whom I will be considering in the next chapter. Both find the new historicist containment thesis too strong while strongly repudiating essentialist humanism, including the essentialist streak in first-generation feminist studies, and both share a commitment to the political present. However, I do think that there is a difference, at times, marked, in the tone and level of antagonism displayed in their respective critiques of new historicism. As we shall see, the cultural materialist mode was often fierce and embattled, but the material feminist mode, at least where new historicism is concerned, seems to be more conciliatory and willing to show an indebtedness to the methods and ideas it helped to foster – and this is especially true of the materialist feminist mode found within the American academy. This, I think, is a legacy of the hostility shown towards new historicism by the first-generation feminists that I have discussed in this chapter. Materialist feminists were perhaps keen not to marginalize 'feminism' from what was increasingly the mainstream of Shakespeare scholarship.

Accordingly, as the 1990s wore on, the distinction between new historicism and materialist feminism became more blurred, as both approaches became more deeply embedded into the critical fabric, and the vitriol of the heated debates of the 1980s faded. Consider, for example, a book such as Jean E. Howard's and Phyllis Rackin's *Engendering a Nation* (1997), seemingly written for the non-specialist, which – somewhat disappointingly given Rackin's own much-more nuanced consideration of the histories, in *Stages of History* (1990)[28] – reasserts the containment thesis in its reading of the history plays, a world in which assertive women represent a threat to order, and in which female subordination and victimization (and even rape) are the inevitable consequence of patriarchal dominance.[29] Here, the union between feminism and new historicism is almost total, to the extent that Peter J. Smith, writing sixteen years later, did not flinch from saying: 'Typical of the New Historicists, Howard and Rackin genuflect submissively in front of the absolute patriarchy of the early modern state'.[30] However, despite this union, as we shall see in the next two chapters, some of the more general underlying problems that the first-generation feminists identified in new historicism, such as the denial agency of individuals and the insufficient theorization of the subject, found support from some unlikely corners of the discipline.

6

The Opponents of New Historicism

What does it mean to be an 'opponent of new historicism'? To answer this question, we must first, to a degree, historicize new historicism itself, because opposing it in the 2000s or 2010s would have carried a very different set of associations from those of the 1980s or 1990s. To put it simply: in the latter case, new historicism was 'new' and represented a challenge, and even threat, to the establishment, whereas in the former, new historicism *seems* to embody the status quo (even if, as we shall see in Chapter 7, in reality it had become supplanted by a de-politicized and de-theorized historicism, somewhat divorced from its 'new' roots). In this chapter, I aim to provide a map of those who have opposed new historicism in both time frames. By necessity the guided tour will be highly selective in order to take in the most salient critiques and will have to range forwards and backwards across this thirty-five-year time span.

Almost from the moment of its birth, new historicism suffered an unusual amount of critical backlash and assessment. This is true to the extent that the body of meta-critical work around new historicism is arguably many times larger than the corpus of new historicist work itself. As Brian Vickers put it: 'Seldom, if ever, has a new and relatively small critical movement (its acknowledged practitioners barely reach a dozen) provoked so much heated discussion in so short a time, with so small a body of achieved work'.[1] Geoffrey Galt Harpham memorably observed that the original critical reception of new historicism was similar to a 'professional wrestling match in which a professional "scientific" wrestler, a gentleman of style and class, makes a few remarkable and ingenious gestures, only eventually to be clubbed senseless by a 450-pound brute'.[2] Such being the case, these are saturated waters and no account could claim to be exhaustive.

In this book so far, I have tended to focus on the first twenty years of new historicist work – the period from 1980 to 2000. There are three reasons for this: first, because this is the period during which the most seminal new historicist studies were produced; second, because these years saw new historicism's dramatic rise and subsequently swift entrenchment as the new critical orthodoxy in Shakespeare studies; and third, perhaps more contentiously, it is difficult to say the extent to which any work has been 'new historicist' since the turn of the twenty-first century, even though the 'opponents of new historicism' appear to multiply. Stephen Greenblatt – as befitting a scholar of his years, status and influence – has courted a more general, mainstream readership, as evidenced by books such as *Will in the World* (2005), a fairly conventional biography by new historicist standards, and the Pulitzer prize-winning *The Swerve* (2012).[3] As is often the case with late works by esteemed and high-profile professors – we might also cite A. D. Nuttall's *Shakespeare: The Thinker* (2007), Marjorie Garber's *Shakespeare After All* (2004), Frank Kermode's *Shakespeare's Language* (2000), or (dare I say) Harold Bloom's *Shakespeare: The Invention of the Human* (1998)[4] – they are enthusiastically received by the broadsheet press and their readership, but are plainly no longer setting the agenda of the discipline. This is not to say that new historicism ceased to be relevant but, rather, to recognize the change in its circumstances. In the 2000s, new historicism – much like New Criticism in the late 1960s – became ingrained, its ideas assumed, its methodologies absorbed; it became the always-already implied de facto

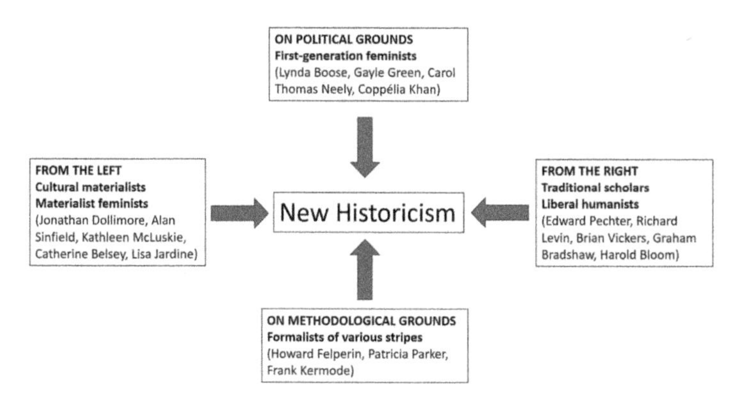

Figure 6.1 *State of play in the 1980s and early 1990s*

mode of criticism. And yet, somewhat paradoxically, it seems to me that during that same period it was an absent centre, because, arguably, there was no longer anyone producing new historicist work.

In the 1980s and 1990s, new historicism at times found itself besieged from all sides. Its historicism upset formalists; its methodological anarchy and indebtedness to post-modern theory rankled with traditional liberal humanist scholars; its apparent political quietude and tendency to view texts as upholding the status quo dissatisfied Marxists and the cultural materialists; and, as we saw in Chapter 5, its focus on men in positions of power drew the ire of feminists. Depending on the critique, new historicism was not historical enough, not literary enough and not political enough to serve. In the diagram (above Figure 6.1) I have attempted to show this visually.

By the 2000s, new historicism had weathered the storm long enough to occupy the aforementioned absent centre, its practitioners suitably honoured. And the number of scholars writing explicitly and avowedly against or at the very least *after* new historicism continues to swell (see Figure 6.2).

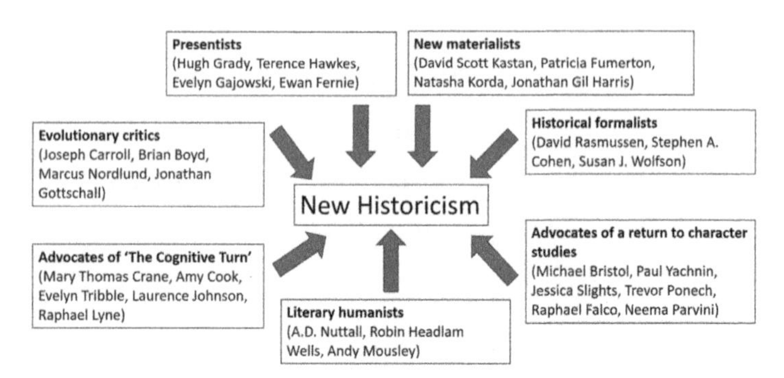

Figure 6.2 *State of play in the 2000s and early 2010s*

Since we discussed the first-generation feminists in Chapter 5, here I will outline the main objections to new historicism, voiced, loosely speaking, by those on 'the right' and on 'the left'.[5] This is complicated slightly by the fact that those on the right – such as Richard Levin, Graham Bradshaw, Edward Pechter and Brian Vickers – had a habit of attacking cultural materialism at the same time as they attacked new historicism. So while British cultural materialists, such as Jonathan Dollimore and Alan Sinfield, were at pains to point out the numerous ways in which they were distinct from their American new historicist counterparts, they often found themselves conflated with them in any case. It is not uncommon to find commentators describing cultural materialism as Jonathan Dollimore's and Alan Sinfield's 'phrase for the new historicism',[6] or the 'British name' for new historicism.[7] Even Howard Felperin, who made a careful and nuanced distinction between cultural poetics and cultural materialism, nevertheless subtitled his chapter on them 'The Two New Historicisms in Renaissance Studies'.[8] For the uninitiated, this conflation can be confusing.

For this reason, I will start with the cultural materialists.[9] As I showed in Chapter 1, the chief theoretical progenitors of new historicism are Clifford Geertz, Michel

Foucault and Hayden White. Cultural materialism, as represented by the work of Jonathan Dollimore and Alan Sinfield, is more firmly rooted in Marxist theory, particularly that of Raymond Williams and Louis Althusser. Like Stephen Greenblatt, at least initially, they set their stall out in the early-modern period. Dollimore's *Radical Tragedy* (1984), and the collection of essays that he edited with Sinfield, *Political Shakespeare* (1985), are the foundational texts of cultural materialism. Much of this early cultural materialist work can be read in contrast to new historicism. Dollimore points out the most crucial difference between the two approaches: 'Did [Shakespeare's] plays reinforce the dominant order, or do they interrogate it to the point of subversion? According to a rough and ready division, new historicists have inclined to the first view, cultural materialists to the second'.[10] As I showed in Chapters 3 and 4, taking their cues from Foucault, even allowing for the subtle developments beyond the hard version of the containment thesis, new historicists tended to see power everywhere, and the scope for genuine subversion as being very difficult, if not impossible. Cultural materialists, meanwhile, armed with Althusser's ideology critique in one hand and Williams's more fluid notions of a fundamentally unstable, contradictory and ever-changing culture in the other, tended instead to see dissidence.

This observation – that new historicists found unbreakable mechanisms of power where cultural materialists found subversion and dissidence – has been made to do much work over the years. But this, I think, papers over more fundamental differences between the two approaches and too readily assumes that they are engaged in the same practice, which I am not convinced they are. As we have seen, new historicist readings tend to anchor themselves in historical anecdotes and to make connections between texts and official ruling ideologies: they use the details of history and text to weave together 'stories'. While they do historicize, it seems to me that cultural materialists employ a great deal more time and space dismantling and repudiating previous criticism and scholarship as being both essentialist humanist and ideological. In much the same way that Althusser tried to purge Marx of Hegel, cultural materialists have tried to purge the study of early modern literature of liberal humanism and 'the sort of criticism which privileges an idealized, context-free 'literature' and, as part of it, constructs [for example] a heroically transcendent "Shakespeare", whose works deal in truths that are true for all time'.[11] When writing about cultural materialism in his book on Stephen Greenblatt, Mark Robson puts it well: 'the declared purpose of such criticism is not to produce more readings of texts, but, instead, to counter traditional readings through a materialist approach to culture'.[12]

In a sense then, cultural materialism is often a kind of meta-critical exercise that acknowledges that a text always-already comes to us as being 'already read'. As Terence Hawkes argues, 'Shakespeare's plays have become one of the central agencies through which our culture performs this operation [...] Shakespeare doesn't mean: *we* mean *by* Shakespeare'[13] (emphasis in original). Cultural materialists thus shift focus from the plays themselves to what people have made of them, because 'it is precisely how and why Shakespeare is read, invoked, praised and affirmed that tell us what has value'.[14] The play becomes a site of ideological and cultural struggle – not only for the 1590s or early 1600s, but also for now. As Felperin observed: 'these critics read and write to change the world, or at least the structure of British society, through the state ideological apparatus of higher education. And unacademic as it may seem to American scholars, they wear their political commitments on their dust jackets'.[15]

For many in the American academy, the political commitment and earnest fervour of cultural materialism – rooted in present concerns – offered a sharp contrast to the arch- and post-ironic tone of new historicism. Thus, arguably the most valuable critiques of new historicism from the left come not from Dollimore or Sinfield (who were busy fighting their own battles with Levin, Vickers et al.) but rather from leftist American scholars looking across the Atlantic and longing for a more politically oriented criticism at home. Several examples of such criticism are valuably collected in the book *Shakespeare Reproduced* (1987), edited by Jean E. Howard and Marion F. O'Connor. Walter Cohen, for example, finds that 'new historicism describes historical difference, but it does not explain historical change'. He also coins a very useful phrase – 'arbitrary connectedness' – to describe the free-ranging way in which new historicists draw links between cultural artefacts and texts. For Cohen, arbitrary connectedness not only 'limits the persuasiveness of much new historicist work' but also serves as the basis for their belief in 'the triumph of containment'. Cohen's main problem is that 'the assumption of arbitrary connectedness seems to preclude a systematic survey of the available evidence, leading instead to a kind of synecdoche in which a single text or group of texts stands in for all texts and thus exhausts the discursive field'.[16] The complaint, it seems, is that new historicists are failing to do their history properly, and in the process end up short-changing the concerns of various political groups by too readily assuming ideological coherence. Where have we heard this before? Cast your mind back to the start of Chapter 3. Traditional historians in the mould of G. R. Elton had very similar objections. As I mentioned in Chapter 4, I am not altogether convinced that it is fair to criticise new historicism on the grounds of its historical accuracy, because it is not at all clear that it has a commitment to any notion of historical truth. It is fairer, I think, to judge it on its own terms: that is, as a method for generating stimulating, original and persuasive new readings of old plays, rather than as a method for producing good (see 'correct' or 'true') history.

Using Cohen's criticisms of 'arbitrary connectedness' and synecdoche as a launch pad, there are several more penetrating critiques (although none of them are by cultural materialists) that get to the heart of the troubled relationship between new historicism and history and politics. Howard Felperin, David Scott Kastan and Richard Lehan have argued – persuasively in my view[17] – that the new historicist use of arbitrary connectedness serves to reproduce formalism at the level of culture and in so doing inadvertently resurrects New Criticism's reverence of the unified whole. This is compounded by its synchronic (as opposed to diachronic) treatment of history. Using the metaphor of a microscope, Felperin explains how new historicism replicates structuralism, and therefore, ironically, cannot hope to 'understand' either history or politics:

> For the new-historicist act of delineating its subject matter along older empirical lines effectively cuts its 'Renaissance' out of the flow of history and turns it into a slice or cross-section of history. This can then be studied, like a slide, under the microscope, where it takes on the aspect of the synchronic system that is certainly culture-specific and conventional [...] but one that has been sealed off from any continuing historical process. For such questions as what 'writes' the culture system under study, and to which culture – Renaissance or contemporary? – it belongs, remain unexplored and largely unasked. The microscope in use was not designed to investigate these matters. To be sure it is no longer 'literature' or 'literary history' that is being isolated as a thing apart – Greenblatt is quite explicit and consistent on this point – but the cultural system within which 'literature' is inscribed. The microscope in use, the method at work, however, is no longer that of historicism – 'empiricist', 'realist', or any other – but of structuralism. And this puts into question the historical status of the enterprise, in so far as it is based on the principle that cultural, like linguistic texts, are to be analysed as synchronic systems [...] My point is [...] that [new historicism] is not genuinely *historical* or seriously political either [...] In approaching Elizabethan culture as a self-contained system of circulating energies cut off from his own cultural system, Greenblatt's cultural poetics relinquishes its potential for an historical understanding that might exert political influence upon the present.[18]

Cultural poetics, therefore, eventually comes to read culture as a unified whole, much as the New Critics read poems as a unified whole. New historicism, it turns out, is another formalism and just as apolitical. In Greenblatt's defence, however, as we saw in Chapter 3, he is keenly aware that there *is* a link between himself and his subject matter – that he sees himself and his concerns reflected back to him in the stories he weaves with the materials of the early modern period. Felperin, I suspect, understands this; but his point is that in viewing the past as *different*, as remote, as cut off from us in the here and now, Greenblatt ensures – ironically, given his professed desire to speak with the dead – that his engagement with the past does not have 'present importance and consequence' beyond an antiquarian interest. In other words, Greenblatt might see himself in the dead, but they don't talk back to him.

Kastan argues along similar lines to those of Felperin; for him, new historicist studies are 'not properly historical at all but rather formalist practices, discovering pattern and order, unity and coherence, in the culture [. . .] exactly as an earlier generation of formalist critics found them in works of literature'.[19] Lehan, meanwhile, teases out the problem of treating history synchronically, and calls instead for a return to the 'the idea of historical process'.[20] And the return to a more conventional, diachronic history would find its culmination in the 2000s, in the work of critics that I have termed 'post-theory historians', such as Douglas Bruster and Patricia Fulmerton, in addition to Kastan himself. I will return to them in Chapter 7.

The cultural materialist concern with the political present would find its ultimate expression in a movement known as presentism, which was spear-headed in the late 2000s and early 2010s by Hugh Grady, Terence Hawkes, Evelyn Gajowski and Ewan Fernie. The aims of this movement are well signalled by the title of a recent collection: *Shakespeare and the Urgency of Now* (2013).[21] Contra-Greenblatt, presentism 'will not yearn to speak with the dead [...] [it] will aim, in the end, to talk to the living'[22] and promise 'a way out of the theoretical thickets of recent years'.[23] While this has been an exciting, almost punkish, development in Shakespeare studies, for the purposes of the present volume – that is, in terms of their critique of new historicism – the presentists, by their own admission, do not build significantly on the cogent criticisms made by Felperin, Kastan or Lehan. Instead, perhaps fittingly, theirs is a genuine attempt to establish a paradigm beyond historicism, rather than dwelling on its shortcomings, often by cheekily reversing its mantras.

However, one crucial respect in which presentists depart from those earlier critiques of new historicism is in their wholesale rejection of historicism itself. Whereas Kastan aims to do the history better than the new historicists, presentists reject the idea that 'history' is what we should be doing in the first place. As Gajowski puts it: 'Presentism departs from attempts on the part of historicism to restore Shakespeare's texts to the conditions of their original production [...] Viewing such a scholarly venture to be a fantasy, presentism focuses instead on the various temporal and geographical conditions in which consumption of Shakespeare's texts occurs'.[24] Grady and Hawkes agree: 'Genuinely to capture, or repeat the past, is fundamentally impossible for a variety of reasons'. Rather than chase a pipe-dream, presentists instead embrace their own inextricable situated-ness in the present because 'we cannot make contact with a past unshaped by our own concerns'.[25] As I have stressed throughout this book so far, I think it is fair to say that, following Hayden White, this was always known to the new historicists, or at least to Greenblatt and Montrose. However, as I shall discuss in Chapter 7, in new historicism's assimilation into critical orthodoxy this little detail appears to have gone missing. In many ways, presentism represents a stronger challenge to the more conventional historicist scholarship carried out in the years after new historicism than it does to the self-consciously post-modern work of Greenblatt and Montrose.

There have been other approaches promising to take us out of the critical doldrums. If you cast your eyes again at Figure 6.2, there are four broad strands of work that have mounted challenges to new historicism (and cultural materialism) on the basis of a renewed focus on human nature, which of course is at odds with much of the anti-humanist theory on which those schools are predicated. At the most extreme end are the evolutionary critics (sometimes called literary Darwinists). Most prominent among these are Joseph Carroll and Brian Boyd, who reject most modern literary theory on the basis that it is a form of social constructionism at odds with the facts of evolutionary science. They do not specifically critique new historicism (or cultural materialism, or deconstruction, or feminist theory), except at this very general level. Their call is for English literature as a discipline to 'wake up at some point and feel the massive overwhelming reality of our own biological existence in the real world'.[26] But the call is for nothing less than a complete break with postmodern theory and an overturn of critical practice so far-reaching that it is extremely unlikely to happen any time soon.

More moderately, although no less forcefully, literary humanists such as Robin Headlam Wells, Andy Mousley and the late A. D. Nuttall have sought to rescue humanism from its pejorative connotations in Shakespeare studies and in so doing restore the '"human interest" element' to his plays.[27] Again, these critics provide not so much critiques of new historicism as a more general dissatisfaction with the fruits of anti-humanist literary theory, of which new historicism is a prominent example. It is a more general bid to restore agency to Shakespeare's texts as well as to the playwright himself. In two elegant passages, Nuttall puts forward the main objections:

> I am suggesting that as soon as you allow the poet cognitive or referential power, we enter into a world of analogy in which the social conditions or composition or, for that matter, the psychological genesis remain palpably distinct

> from the achieved work. The *root* is not the flower [...] New Historicism now holds sway in universities in Britain and North America (though there are signs that its grip is weakening). Where 'Historicism' means expending all one's attention on the immediate historical circumstances of composition and seeking to explicate the work in terms of those circumstances, I am opposed. The argument of this book is that, although knowledge of the historical genesis can on occasion illumine a given work, the greater part of the artistic achievement of our best playwright is internally generated. It is the product, not of his time, but of his own, unresting, creative intelligence.[28]

Nuttall, Wells and Mousley can all be seen as seeking to return to a more 'literary' engagement with Shakespeare's works.

Somewhat related to this development has been the re-emergence of character study, which seeks to restore agency not only to texts but also to the characters who populate them. Again, the challenge to new historicism comes from a general complaint about its consequences rather than a specific critique, namely that it has encouraged us to think about characters as ideological constructs rather than as representations of real people. Proponents of a renewed interest in character include Michael Bristol, Paul Yachnin and Jessica Slights; my own recent work has also proceeded in this vein.[29] And finally there has been the 'cognitive turn', in the work of scholars such as Mary Thomas Crane, Evelyn Trimble and Amy Cook, which seeks to bring developments in neuroscience and cognitive psychology to bear on the study of Shakespeare's plays.[30] All these movements signal a general wind of change – a swinging back of the critical pendulum – away from context and culture, and towards text and the individual.

Let us turn now to a rather different set of voices, broadly speaking, to those who have attacked new historicism from the right. They belong to a host of figures that should by now be familiar to readers of this book: Richard Levin,

Graham Bradshaw, Brian Vickers and Edward Pechter – the four horsemen. These critics are all, with varying degrees of vehemence, hostile to post-modern theory; typically they set themselves against not only new historicism but also cultural materialism, deconstruction, feminism and any other approach that draws significantly from continental philosophy. They paint themselves as being bastions of common sense and scholarly standards against what Bradshaw calls the '"ismic" tagging', which 'is a familiar but anticritical feature of contemporary academic criticism'.[31] To capture their mindset, I can again rely on Nuttall for a good quotation:

> I have always 'leaned against the wind'. *A New Mimesis*, when it first came out, certainly did not give readers what they wanted to hear. In the early 1980s, 'Theory' (with a capital T) reigned supreme. The tendency of this movement, quite inescapably, was to resolve substance into relation, to weaken the notion of factual truth. Realism in art was itself reconstrued as a tissue of conventions. Of course, there were always choice spirits who held out for common sense [...] I remember a conversation with a friend in which he suggested that we should have our names inscribed on some not easily accessible stone, high on an ancient building (one covered by a preservation order), together with the legend 'We never believed in Theory'.[32]

It is fair to say that Levin, Bradshaw and Vickers might all have been happy signatories (Pechter perhaps less so). They are warranted space here because, much like G. R. Elton in the 'History' department, they were each prepared to express opinions (often polemically) that many of their colleagues and peers held privately or at any rate were not willing to put into print.

All four produced sustained critiques of new historicism. Edward Pechter's essay 'The New Historicism and Its Discontents' (1987) – perhaps owing to its publication in the prominent and widely read journal *PMLA* and the fact that it came first – has arguably been the most widely cited. Richard Levin, whose several essays attacking new historicism, written in the early 1990s, are collected in *Looking for An Argument* (2003) – a book which read today uncannily brings to mind the attention-seeking of the internet troll. Brian Vickers, never less than acidic, included a lengthy chapter on new historicism in *Appropriating Shakespeare* (1993), a book in which he also takes to task deconstruction, psychoanalysis, feminism and seemingly every other approach born in the late 1970s and early 1980s. In the same year, Graham Bradshaw published *Misrepresentations* (1993), which was a similar broadside against recent critical approaches, with special attention devoted to new historicism and cultural materialism. Rather than work through these polemics individually, for the sake of convenience I will distil their vitriol into a set of bullet points. This is not to say that these four critiques are identical; but they land many of the same punches, and I imagine that each one would nod approvingly at any point of criticism provided by any other that was missing in their own account.

I have organized the chief objections to new historicism from these four objectors in five main areas. These critics contend that new historicism:

1 Is not 'new' but in fact guilty of many of the same tendencies as the old historicism. Despite some obvious differences between them and E. M. W. Tillyard and his generation, they nonetheless construct an 'imaginary and monolithic audience',[33] and in so doing rely on the 'same basic assumptions' as old historicists.[34]

2 In homogenizing Elizabethan culture in this way, compounded by its Foucauldian obsession with power it systematically denies agency to individuals as well as to literary texts. 'The flow is markedly one way, from culture to literary text, and the effect [...] is to privilege the cultural text as the stable and determining

point of reference'.[35] This is, in other words, the problem of the hard containment thesis.

3 Has a 'disregard for the integrity of the literary text'.[36] Its practitioners 'do not infer their interpretation from the dramatic facts and then relate it to the history of the period but proceed in the reverse order. They begin with their interpretation of this history, which is based on very high-level generalizations that are treated as unproblematic and unmediated, and descend from it to their historical interpretation of the play, which fits the play into this history, and from there to the dramatic facts, that are mediated (i.e. transformed) by these prior operations'.[37]
4 Produces 'bad' history because it is guilty of the 'bending of evidence, background and foreground, to suit one-sided interpretations'.[38]
5 Is anachronistic because it is guilty of 'the foisting of modern cultural and political attitudes on to Renaissance texts'.[39]

Despite their contentiousness at the time, many of these criticisms have since become standard charges brought against new historicism (along with those articulated by Felperin, Lehan and Kastan). In Chapters 3 and 4, I considered all five charges when putting some of the seminal new historicist works to scrutiny. And it is not unfair to suggest that all five have proven to be, at least to some extent, true. However, I would make a qualification for each of them as follows:

1 While it is true that the logic of the typical new historicist essay seems to rest on a monolithic culture, when one reads across several new historicists essays – often even by the same author – one finds that each of them constructs a slightly different version of early-modern culture. Bradshaw, Levin and Vickers all complain about the number of contradictions between new historicist accounts, but it is curious to also

charge them with imposing a monolithic version of culture. They are right to say that *within* each account, we find a monolithic culture, but I am suggesting that across multiple accounts we find different monolithic *cultures* (see also my account of the new historicist readings of *Measure for Measure* in Chapter 4).

2 It is especially true of early new historicist work that the hard version of the containment thesis seemed to preclude virtually all agency for both the individual and the text. But later work, especially by Greenblatt and Montrose (see Chapter 3), conceived of a much more nuanced and reciprocal relationship between individuals and their cultures.

3 This point largely stands; new historicism's unique selling point was never in its close textual reading, to which, after all, it was meant to serve as antidote. Its drawing card was transforming texts by focusing on contexts.

4 Again this stands, but as I've said (see Chapters 1, 3 and 4) it is not clear to me that new historicists ever had any intention of producing 'good' history, in the conventional sense. It is 'new' precisely because it is a departure from the old evidenced-based positivist-objectivist history.

5 Once again, this stands, but it seems to me that new historicists – especially Greenblatt and Montrose – are entirely aware of this.

In every case, excepting perhaps the first, the charges brought against new historicists are 'crimes' of which they are already aware.

We have come to a impasse. It seems to me that new historicists stand accused by these critics simply of *being new historicists*. Levin, Vickers and Bradshaw – to put it very plainly – do not think that new historicism is a very effective way of reading literary texts, and, really, when push comes to shove, would prefer there to be no new historicists. For them, scholarly standards have been established for a reason. Claims about history demand evidence. Dramatic texts have 'knowable facts' that one can get right or wrong, as does history itself. For Vickers and Levin it is simply *wrong* to read *The Tempest* (for example) in a colonial context, because the known facts (of history, of the details of the play) simply cannot support such a reading.[40] They abhor the new historicist habit of working through analogy, because it contravenes the facts. In such a world of absolutes, in which scholarship is either right or wrong, it is difficult to see the scope for a variety of approaches beyond the demands of traditional scholarship. And, of course, since they appeared to be against seemingly every critical approach that is not traditional scholarship, perhaps this is exactly what Vickers, Levin and their ilk wanted. In my view, this is to judge new historicism unfairly, because it is to hold it to a set of scholarly standards from which it has professed to break.

I draw a distinction between *scholars*, on the one hand, and *critics* on the other.[41] The drive of scholars is towards accuracy, the drive of critics is towards insight and originality. Stephen Greenblatt – like G. Wilson Knight, or A. P. Rossiter before him – is a great *critic*. A gifted and imaginative interpreter of Shakespeare's plays, and other literary texts, with the ability to turn commonplace readings on their head and provoke much discussion about what is at stake in them. It helps that he writes with flair. To accuse him of bad *scholarship* is, in my view, to miscast him, and indeed the place of new historicism itself, in the history of Shakespeare studies. Wasn't new historicism, after all, meant to strike fear into '[c]onventional scholars – entrenched, self-absorbed, protective of guild loyalties and turf, specialized in the worst senses'?[42] As discussed in Chapter 4, I think the problem comes from a lay understanding of the term 'historicism', which sets up so many expectations of G. R. Elton-style positivism as embodied in a great literary historian like E. K. Chambers. Greenblatt never claimed to be the second coming of Chambers. New historicism is best understood not as a form of literary history but rather as a form of literary *criticism*: as an approach that generates new and insightful readings. Even a cantankerous Frank Kermode conceded: '[even though] New Historicists haven't really given enough thought to history [...] [t]he best practitioners escape this charge, not because they espouse superior versions of the New Historicism, but because, even willy-nilly, they say something interesting about [...] what used to be called literature'.[43] At its very best it can be transformative, because the links – made through arbitrary connections and wild leaps of logic without any basis in the 'real' evidence – unlock new and unusual contexts for Shakespeare's plays and, with them, previously-unthought-of avenues of discussion. This is new historicism's great contribution to the field, but – as I will elaborate in the next chapter – I fear that those of a more scholarly mindset, those who care more about accuracy than insight or originality, did not recognize this. And so, with time, came the drive towards 'correcting' new historicism's methodical anarchy – perceived as a shortcoming – with a more corrective, scholarly and basically old-fashioned and antiquarian form of historicism. And with that drive, much of the imagination, dynamism and originality was lost. Although it seems absurd to say so, viewed from this perspective, the likes of Vickers, Levin and Bradshaw may have lost many battles but, in the long-term, won the war.

7

The Legacy of New Historicism

> We – members of the current generation of graduate students – can without any distortion of fact be labelled children of New Historicism. Stephen Greenblatt's *Renaissance Self-Fashioning* was first published in 1980, four years before either of us were born. Granted, we may be some of the younger academics out there, but the fact that New Historicism has, quite literally, been around longer than we have makes a strong case for the need for a new set of critical practices.[1]

So Rebecca Munson and Claude Willan begin a disarmingly candid essay – it was two years before I was born too! I will quote from their essay a little more:

> Part of our Master's course consisted of seminars with academics from the Oxford faculty in which they would share with us their routes into the profession [...] One such seminar [...] was not [...] a positive experience. Given halfway through the year by an academic, who, in the short time since receiving a doctorate had published three books, our group of Master's students was told that to succeed in academia we ought to adhere to a methodological orthodoxy. This orthodoxy was not simply

> historicist literary study but an interdisciplinary literary historiography. Both of us felt compelled to ask our professor whether this wasn't somehow wrong-headed, whether telling graduate students that to study literature with professional success they had to prepare to use it as a lens through which to examine historical circumstance wasn't a little defeatist about the possibility of genuinely literary study. Our questions were not answered, and the seminar moved on. But those questions stayed with us, and the seminars and conferences we attended at Oxford continued to endorse the study of literature with historical goals. We both wondered: how had it come about that the prevailing literary hegemony was one which shied away from, well, literature?[2]

I too studied for a Master's at Oxford, and I too, struck by this sometimes profoundly unreflexive adherence to orthodoxy, found myself wondering – overwhelmingly – exactly the same question. And this strongly motivated the direction of my own work. It seems that every generation feels a little trapped by the prevailing dominant mode. The new historicists had felt stifled by the New Critics (who themselves had felt constrained by an older generation of literary historians), and likewise those of us born in the early 1980s cannot help but yearn for [...] well, something *else*.

And so it is that every critical approach has a natural shelf life – apparently about thirty years. Throughout this book we have encountered many commentators who sounded the death knell for new historicism. Some were very premature (for example, Edward Pechter in 1987 or Howard Felperin in 1990); others (David Scott Kastan in 1999 or Douglas Bruster in 2003) were closer to the point at which new historicism ceased to be such a prominent force in Shakespeare studies, even if it was still true, as Michael L. Hays said at the time, that 'New Historicists rule English departments and professional organizations, and not yet from the grave'.[3] As I shall discuss in this chapter, those critical of new historicism came successfully to supplant it with their own brands of historicism. However, it was 2012 – as it turns out thirty years since new historicism was labelled as such by Greenblatt[4] – that saw a slew of books reassessing historicism: *Rethinking Historicism from Shakespeare to Milton* edited by Anne Baines Coiro and Thomas Fulton, *The Limits of Literary Historicism* edited by Allen Dunn and Thomas F. Haddox, which contains the aforementioned essay by Munson and Willan, and two books by the present author, *Shakespeare's History Plays: Rethinking Historicism*, and *Shakespeare and Contemporary Theory: New Historicism and Cultural Materialism*. As Ian Frederick Moulton put it in a recent review: 'new historicism was bound to get old soon or later [...] Since the mid-1980s historicism has been the dominant discourse in early modern literary studies. That it is under attack for being outmoded or hegemonic thirty years later is not surprising'.[5]

In the introduction to their volume, Dunn and Haddox accuse historicists of becoming complacent and formulaic:

> New Historicism is now no longer new, but in the process of becoming established, it has lost even the minimal degree of critical reflection about its premises that we saw in [Harold Aram] Veeser's polemics. By treating these premises as beyond challenge and too self-evident to require explanation, historicist criticism has produced an abundance of formulaic, complacent readings of literary texts and failed to explain just what historicism's deepest commitments are and why they continue to matter. Too often, it has become just what [Alan] Liu described back in 1989: a "narcissistic, *in*disciplinary nostalgia for subversion that is the secret indulgence lurking within *inter*disciplinary cultural study".[6]

There is an interesting and perhaps even unconscious shift in the language of this passage. 'New historicism' quietly becomes merely 'historicist criticism'. Is it simply that it has been around long enough for the 'new' to be no longer valid, or does it reflect a more substantial change in the type of work being produced in Shakespeare studies?

It seems to me that, since the turn of the twenty-first century, new historicism has been silently usurped by a much plainer form of historicism stripped of its theoretical underpinnings and of any tendencies that might be considered methodologically renegade. Theory was dismissed as old hat, and with this dismissal the self-reflexive theorizing that had marked the debates of the 1980s simply stopped. And thus we come to the myopic attitude that Munson and Willian encountered in their unnamed professor at Oxford. By the late 1990s, the excitement that new historicism and cultural materialism had generated had long since faded. Witness, for example, Gordon McMullan's colourless preface to the collection *Renaissance Configurations* (1998), a piece written so dispassionately that it takes on a certain clinical quality:

> *Renaissance Configurations* is a collection of essays on cultural formations in early modern England which focuses on questions of gender, sexuality and politics in the relations of public and private, verbal and spatial, material and textual [...] No single, monolithic approach is represented, though: the differences between the essays are as important as the similarities and congruences, and there is a conscious pluralism of agenda and attitude throughout. It is this heterogeneity, this diversity of focus, that most clearly differentiates the present volume from the representative collections of the mid-1980s [...] The present volume has *less specificity, is less politically focused* [...] *Renaissance Configurations* expresses the contributors' desire to produce work that is [...] both 'scholarly' and 'theoretical'; in other words to perform cultural criticism from the perspective of philosophical, anthropological and political critique, but *always in ways that can be demonstrated to be both historically and textually appropriate.*[7] (emphasis mine)

So to tease out what McMullan is saying: the contributors do not stand for anything in particular, wish to ease off from discussing anything too political, and wish to marry their 'cultural criticism' (a somewhat soft, non-committal and nebulous term) with what amounts to the tools of conventional scholarship. This is a profoundly conservative retreat to the safety of traditional literary history. It is difficult to imagine a Brian Vickers or Richard Levin – or indeed anyone – writing furious polemics in response to so tame a statement. We are a long way from the heyday of new historicism here, and it was clear that something had changed.

The turn of the new millennium saw the publication of two key studies which helped to hasten the replacement of new historicism with new, more scholarly alternatives. These were: *Renaissance Culture and the Everyday* (1999) edited by Patricia Fumerton and Simon Hunt, which announced 'a new new historicism', and *Shakespeare After Theory* (1999), David Scott Kastan's sustained attack on new historicism, which he sought to replace with what he jokingly labelled 'The New Boredom': 'a greater delight in particularity'.[8] Although each of these works claims to build from new historicism, what they each propose in practice amounts to a complete dismantling of the historiographical approach I outlined in Chapter 1. Collectively, we might call these critics 'post-theory historicists', or 'everyday historicists', although the preferred term has become 'new materialists'. In what follows, I will briefly consider the contributions of these two books and their legacy.

Fumerton's introduction to *Renaissance Culture and the Everyday* starts memorably with a passage about the early modern practice – to modern eyes, barbaric – of torturing pigs and other livestock before cooking and eating them 'to render their flesh more tender and tempting'.[9] She follows up by reprinting a harrowing recipe for roasting a goose alive and registering how its author took visible delight in the pain and suffering of the animal. It is a deliberate echo of the Greenblattian anecdote, but her intention is to employ it to different ends:

> But the new historicism of the '80s generally employed such common subjects to very uncommon ends: as prolegomena to discussions of royalty, the courts, the state, and (male) power. In a word, it was 'political' historicism [...] Even new historicism's more 'grounded' British counterpart, cultural materialism, worked primarily in this lofty political mode [...] My more modest reading of anecdotes about daily culinary violence [...] is a bird of a different feather. It characterizes a new breed of '90s new historicism. This newly emergent new historicism focuses primarily on the common, but the common in both a class and cultural sense: the low (common people), the ordinary (common speech, common wares, common sense), the familiar (common known), the customary or typical or taken-for-granted (common law, commonplace, communal), etc.[10]

The influence of Fernand Braudel here is palpable, although it is indirect, coming by way of the cultural theorist Michel de Certeau's *The Practice of Everyday Life*.[11] Fumerton presents this 'second generation' of new historicists as working to update rather than replace their forebears. The singular anecdote as synecdoche – as per the criticisms I outlined in Chapter 6 – is seen as problematic and replaced by 'multifarious supporting details'. The textualism of the older new historicism, along with its focus on ideology or matrixes of power relations, is replaced with the material and physical. And perhaps more excitingly, following de Certeau, the top-down model of a society controlled and contained by an all-persuasive dominant power is challenged by a bottom-up model in which 'in his or her daily practices, the common person tactically and almost invisibly transforms from within the social structures he or she inhabits'.[12] Braudel, who as you will recall, argued that 'hardly anything changed at all' at this every-day level for almost 400 years,[13] would have no doubt found such claims optimistic. Nonetheless, the essays collected in *Renaissance Culture and the Everyday* remain fascinating, and, in many ways, this version of new historicism rings truer to the claims of writing 'counterhistory' than its 1980s counterpart – and with their spinning out of ever-new contexts, the essays owe something to the method pioneered by Leah Marcus in *Puzzling Shakespeare* that I considered in Chapter 4.

That does not mean, however, that the volume is without its shortcomings. The most penetrating critique of its approach is found in Douglas Bruster's *Shakespeare and the Question of Culture* (2003), in which he traces how Fumerton's use of 'materialism' represents a complete break with its traditional Marxist connotations. It is fair to say that Bruster spots a disconcerting literal-mindedness in much of this work, which he demonstrates by homing in on a passage by Deborah Shuger found in the first essay in the collection. It reads:

> These essays began as an attempt to document an hypothesis that turned out to be false. While preparing a course on early modern autobiography, I ran across an intriguing essay by Georges Gusdorf which hypothesized that the invention of the clear glass mirror in the sixteenth century gave rise to modern, reflexive self-consciousness, which, in turn, led to the sudden proliferation of autobiographical genres. I thought it might be worthwhile to trace the role this novel everyday artifact played in the emergence of early modern selfhood; at the time it seemed a plausible and suitably materialist alternative to current narratives of the modern self as a capitalist epiphenomenon.[14]

Bruster seizes on the last sentence:

> This sentence is worth lingering over, if for no other reason that it stunningly overturns conventional definitions of materialism and conventional assumptions about materialist practice. With twenty-three words, Shuger dispenses of almost two centuries of materialist philosophy and criticism. She suggests here that reading Renaissance mirrors is a 'suitably materialist alternative' to seeing the

> modern self as 'a capitalist epiphenomenon', but does not inform her readers about a sticky bit of nomenclature. That is, studies that focus on the epiphenomenon of capitalism are, of course, Marxist works, works traditionally defined as 'materialist' criticism [...] I have paid this paragraph so much attention because it contains within it something like the whole project of the new materialism. We have, in this sentence, not only the separation from Marx and an implicit argument that Marxist criticism is not truly materialist at base; we also have the assumption that only things that can be held or touched are the legitimate focus of 'materialism'.[15]

This is an unwitting return to the vulgar materialism of the mid-nineteenth century, which of course predated Marx. Although Bruster does not say so explicitly, we are perhaps here witnessing what happens when practice is favoured so absolutely over theory: theoretical slippages, or, worse, theoretical amnesia.

Renaissance Culture and the Everyday contains precisely zero references to Louis Althusser, which is curious when one recalls that for him 'ideology has a material existence' and weaves itself invisibly in the very everyday practices that Fumerton outlines.[16] Ideology manifests itself as the same 'taken-for-granted' 'common sense' practices that are supposed to represent its transformation. From the Althusserian perspective, it is difficult to see how these early modern men and women going about their everyday life – 'working by themselves' one might say – are 'invisibly transforming' their societies. Surely such 'busy work' is what has ensured over the centuries that the masses of the *longue durée* have not rebelled? Capitalism reproduces itself by distracting its subjects for long enough that they never think about their actual conditions – this is Marxism 101. But the so-called 1990s new historicists see instead a kind of people power in consumerism, in which individuals – much like the troubled protagonist of Chuck Palahniuk's *Fight Club* – appear to identify absolutely with the objects around them. Bruster's suspicion is that this work is driven not by any theoretical impetus but by 'the impulse to lecture on an object or anecdote in a masterful, controlling way'. For him it 'hints at [a] critical fetishism [...] that, in replacing the large with small and the intangible with what is capable of being touched or held, threatens to restrict the new materialism's usefulness as cultural and historical explanation', and 'runs the risk of being seen as a tchotchke criticism'.[17] My own concern, along similar lines, is that it gives rise to the critic-as-museum-curator; that the larger intellectual questions of literary criticism – raised, for example, by Shakespeare's endlessly complex plays – are subordinated to the smaller (see also academic, trivial) questions of antiquarianism raised by the curio. It is work marked by diligent scholarship rather than critical insight. While such work can be extraordinarily interesting not to mention rewarding in itself, it should not come at the expense of literary criticism itself.[18]

The turn from theory to historical practice is even more marked in Kastan's *Shakespeare After Theory*. He claims that he 'does not want to engage here in New Historicism bashing', but, despite a footnote pre-emptively countering this charge, Kastan does spend much of his time doing just that. He accuses new historicist works of 'narcissism' and with being 'too overtly self-interested to be compelling as historical accounts'. A 'paradox', which, he says, 'emerges [...] not from their historical naïveté but from their theoretical sophistication'. For Kastan, the new historicist focus on strategies of power is too abstract to serve, and, in finding 'social life to be as well wrought as any poem', ultimately (as per the critique I outlined in Chapter 6) came to replicate the formalism of the New Critics. He would prefer 'a more rigorously historical' practice:[19]

> a sharper focus on the material relations of discourse to the world in which it circulates would give its cultural analysis more historical purchase, fixing it more firmly in relation to the actual producers and consumers of those discourses,

> locating it, that is, in the world of lived history. Only then is discourse truly enlivened, recognized as a product of human desire and design.[20]

And this can only be achieved by 'turning to history from theory'.

Kastan anticipates three objections to this suggested turn by offering three corresponding counter-arguments. I will consider each of them presently. The first objection is that, in making this turn, Kastan 'returns literary studies to the positivism of an older, untheoretical historiography'.[21] To counter this, he argues that while (*a la* Hayden White, see Chapter 1) we cannot access the past except in mediated form, it still *existed*, and this in itself lends value to our reconstructions of it. This is a rather unsatisfactory counter to the charge. Recall the passage that I quoted from G. R. Elton in Chapter 1 in which he argued that his work 'embodies an assumption that the study and writing of history are justified in themselves, and reflects a suspicion that a philosophic concern with such problems as the reality of historical knowledge or the nature of historical thought only hinders the practice of history'.[22] It is difficult to see how Kastan's position, including his pre-emptive defence, is not, however mediated, a return to this point of view.

The second possible objection that Kastan apprehends is that, in its demand for rare books and difficult-to-access archival materials, his proposed return to an evidence-first approach to history 'returns the study of literature to an elitism it has struggled to escape'. To counter this, he argues that if one is to 'ignore the processes and practices by which the literary work is produced and read, we are left with an honorific and toothless formalism that offers in exchange for its apparently democratic principle of access a profound lack of consequence for literary study'. This is a bold statement and needs to be interrogated more closely. It seems that, for Kastan, a text cannot connote if it is removed from its 'necessary conditions of production', to so remove it is to 'rob it of its actual ties to a social world of meaningful and multiple human agency'.[23] Is it possible that Kastan has forgotten about the true power of literature? That readers and theatre-goers 'lose themselves' in its characters and situations? Teenagers reading *The Catcher in the Rye* today need not transport themselves back to the 1950s in order to 'see themselves' in Holden Caulfield. Can we really, without being hopelessly elitist, dismiss their experience as a 'toothless formalism'? And what exactly do we need to understand about the 'necessary conditions' that produced a play like *Hamlet* to invest ourselves in the psycho-drama and its mysteries? 'The *root* is not the flower'.[24] It seems to me that Kastan's absolute insistence on a 'more rigorously historical' approach to literature *does* return us to the ivory tower, in divorcing the study of literature from the very thing that led so many people to fall in love with it in the first place. It is the very opposite of democratizing.

But there is a more troubling claim made by Kastan's statement: namely, that work which doesn't try to explicate these 'necessary conditions' has a 'profound lack of consequence'. Why? How? For whom? By whose criteria? This was the sort of position that Howard Felperin foresaw in 1990:

> To accept [...] relativism [...] would be not only to abandon the 'struggle', but to invite extinction at the hands of a dominant culture only too ready to dismiss all historical and literary studies as a luxury society can no longer afford. How much easier for it to do so when the 'knowledge' derived by the latter is only a 'reading', a matter of opinion or interpretation. Whether one is interested primarily in the political or the philosophical dimensions of historical texts – or sees them as inextricable – the problem of 'conventionalism', with its inescapable relativism, looms large at a moment when the value of studying those texts within an increasingly reactionary culture is an open question.[25]

Kastan's apparent dismissal of any study that is not working to 'advance knowledge' through yet further and further historical exposition has the distinct undertone of the reactionary culture that Felperin describes. This is literary criticism – or rather literary historical, empirical scholarship – as social utility. It seems that for Kastan there is simply no value without such utility. Ten years later, Hugh Grady noted that while Kastan 'has always been careful to credit and indeed utilize many of the ideas and outcomes of critical theory, 'others in the field have been less scrupulous, and it is evident that in some circles in Shakespeare studies there is a feeling that positivist scholarship has been vindicated and that the age of theory was an unaccountable and regrettable lapse in a now-restored, facts-laden tradition'.[26] And this is perhaps the inevitable consequence of calling for a turn to history from theory – the nuances and qualifications get lost along the way. This has real consequences. It dictates the funding decisions of Arts Councils. It dictates the hiring decisions of English departments. Left unchecked, Andrew Hadfield's concern that the return to positivist scholarship – and the continued proliferation of work in this vein – is 'running the risk of transforming the discipline of English into a branch of History, of making literary criticism just one minor form of cultural history' will come to fruition.[27]

Finally, and we have glimpsed this already, there is the objection that Kastan's proposed 'focus on history [...] deflects attention from the literary text itself'. In his counter, Kastan problematizes the category of the 'text itself', which he argues is an idealization that 'never exists apart from the various materializations that have made it present'. We must recognize that 'a play's materializations, in the printing house and in the playhouse, *are* the play's meanings'.[28] Once again, I must ask: meanings for whom? And are the meanings of literary texts really locked into a frieze and tied to the moment of their gestation in this way? Is there no such thing as 'the philosophical'? Must ideas always be so fixed inextricably to particular materials in a particular time and place in this way? This is a hard materialism that seems not to allow even for universalized *concepts*. And yet, to make any sense of the plays, the essays that form the middle section of Kastan's book must rest ultimately on such concepts. Indeed, it is difficult to see how his conclusions about the plays – for example, that 'the histories expose idealizations of political power by presenting rule as role, by revealing that power passes to him who can best control and manipulate the visual and verbal symbols of authority'[29] – derive immanently from his assorted historical facts rather than from assiduous close readings of 'the text itself'.

Since 1999, we have seen new directions for historicist work. There have been three broad strains. The first, generally speaking, acknowledged an indebtedness to new historicism, but turned from its focus on early modern power structures and their subjects to *objects* – that is real, material objects, the stuff of everyday life. This approach can be seen as the logical extension of that pioneered in *Renaissance Culture and the Everyday*; its most excellent practitioners have been Jonathan Gil Harris and Natasha Korda.[30] At its very best, this work can be exhilarating, and bring to mind the experience of reading Fernand Braudel (see Chapter 1). A second strain is more in line with the culturally-focused approach for which Bruster has argued: 'thin description' rather than 'thick description'.[31] Some, such as Peter Grav, have called this the 'new economic criticism', in which 'the focus seems fixed on broader economic trends and events, such as the usury debate and Tudor currency debasement, rather than what some perceive as the narrower focus of much New Historicist writing' and in which 'diachronic readings, rather than synchronic, are emphasized'.[32] This work is more strongly informed by Marxist theory than the other strains and has produced some very interesting readings of Shakespeare's plays. A third strain can be seen in the field of editing, in which, since the early 1990s, following the work of Peter Stallybrass and Margareta De Grazia – and much to the chagrin of our old friend Edward Pechter – there has been a significant resurgence of interest in materiality of texts.[33] This work has done much to destabilize literary categories, such as word, work, character and author, which have been taken for granted in the past, and shown them to be editorial constructions that post-date Shakespeare by at least 200 years.

As may be clear by now, despite their various claims to be indebted to new historicism, the indebtedness is difficult to detect in these movements, beyond a general orientation towards historical context (even if it is no doubt true that few of them could have existed had new historicism not taken place). 'New materialist' work strips out the renegade charm that in the 1980s gave new historicism much of its vitality, and replaces it with scholarly conventionalism, often delivered in a corrective mode that its new historicist progenitors seldom adopted. That new historicism was not built to last should not come as a surprise, however, because its practitioners never claimed to be much more than a rag-tag collection of brilliant mavericks who were retroactively grouped together under a hasty label. The banner 'new historicism' went on to become perhaps the most successful branding exercise that the discipline has ever known, such that its presence has been felt long after the point that its light went out. And we have seen subsequent groups of critics try to repeat that success with similar branding exercises ('presentism', 'new new historicism', and so on).

So, with all of this said, what is 'the legacy of new historicism' in Shakespeare studies? In my view it constitutes the following six categories:

1. A radical and provocative questioning of the principles and assumptions that underpin traditional scholarly work (whether formalist or historicist).
2. The introduction to Shakespearean discourse of theoretical concepts, especially those inherited from Michel Foucault.
3. A will to look beyond the isolated text at the multiple contexts – even unlikely ones – that inform the production of any work of literature.

4 A shift in focus from language and form, or characters and their motivations, to representations of power, politics and history.
5 A shift in perception about Shakespeare's works (and literary works in general), from the belief that they are timeless and universal to the belief that they are wholly historically contingent.
6 Correspondingly, a de-privileging of literature as a 'special' category of text. Literary works are cultural artefacts, no different from maps, pamphlets, instruction manuals, items of clothing, or any number of everyday objects.

British cultural materialists and the materialist feminists would also build on new historicist work to add a seventh:

7 A renewed focus on identity politics, and a radical questioning of the Dead-White-Male patriarchy.

Even if new historicism itself is no longer being practised, these seven broad categories, in some shape or form, have endured to the present day. It is why graduates of the past decade can still realistically call themselves 'children of New Historicism'. It is also why, no matter which way the critical pendulum swings in the coming years, new historicism has left an indelible mark on Shakespeare studies that shook it to its foundations.

Even if the new materialists did not intend their version of Shakespeare studies 'after Theory' to lapse into a common-sense positivist historicism, to some extent this is what has transpired. Though there have been exceptional 'new materialist' studies produced in the past fifteen years, the same time frame has seen an excess of work that has been leaden and formulaic, almost rote, in its complacent adherence to the prevailing orthodoxies. Hopefully, however, the most enduring legacy of new historicism will be its original spirit: that stubborn and probing resistance to staid orthodoxy and easy assumptions that we might call the will towards the 'new'.

NOTES

Chapter 1

1 Jean-Paul Sartre, *What Is Literature?*, trans. Bernard Fretchman (New York: Philosophical Library, 1947), 74.

2 First quoted in Neema Parvini, 'The Scholars and The Critics: Shakespeare Studies and Theory in the 2010s', *Shakespeare* 10 (2) (Spring 2014): 212.

3 Jean E. Howard, 'The New Historicism in Renaissance Studies', *English Literary Renaissance* 16 (1) (December 1986): 19.

4 Fredric Jameson, *Postmodernism, or, The Cultural Logic of Late Capitalism* (Durham, NC: University of Duke Press, 1991), 189.

5 Catherine Gallagher and Stephen Greenblatt, *Practising New Historicism* (Chicago, IL and London: University of Chicago Press, 2000), 3, 18, 2.

6 See Terry Eagleton, *After Theory* (London: Allen Lane, 2003); Valentine Cunningham, *Reading After Theory* (Malden, MA and Oxford: Blackwell, 2002); David Scott Kastan, *Shakespeare After Theory* (New York and London: Routledge, 1999) and, at least a decade ahead of the curve, Thomas Docherty, *After Theory: Postmodernism/Postmarxism* (New York and London: Routledge, 1990).

7 See Douglas Bruster, *Shakespeare and the Question of Culture: Early Modern Literature and the Cultural Turn* (New York and London: Palgrave Macmillan, 2003), 'While some observers would see new historicism as a kind of ghost [...] I believe that such characterizations overstate the case. New historicism can be seen as a thing of the past precisely because so many of its assumptions and practices have become standard and hence less valuable', 29.

8 Kastan, *Shakespeare After Theory,* 18.

9 David Simpson, 'Touches of the Real', *London Review of Books* 23 (10) (May 2001): 25.

10 See Neema Parvini, *Shakespeare's History Plays: Rethinking Historicism* (Edinburgh: Edinburgh University Press, 2012a), esp. 10–32, 52–83, and, albeit to a lesser extent, *Shakespeare and Contemporary Theory: New Historicism and Cultural Materialism* (New York and London: Bloomsbury, 2012b), esp. 97–121.

11 See Gallagher and Greenblatt, *Practising New Historicism,* 2.

12 Harold Aram Veeser, 'The New Historicism', in *The New Historicism Reader*, ed. Harold Aram Veeser (New York and London: Routledge, 1994a), 12.

13 See Dominick LaCapra, 'Rethinking Intellectual History and Reading Texts', *History and Theory* 19 (3) (October 1980): 245–76; *Rethinking Intellectual History: Texts, Contexts, Language* (Ithaca, NY: Cornell University Press, 1983); *History and Criticism* (Ithaca, NY: Cornell University Press, 1985); for an argument for his importance to literary studies see Suzanne Gearhart, 'History as Criticism: The Dialogue of History and Literature', *Diacritics* 17 (3) (Autumn 1987): 56–65.

14 Fredric Jameson, *The Political Unconscious*, 2nd edn (1982; New York and London: Routledge, 2002), ix.

15 See Stephen Greenblatt, ed., *New World Encounters*, (Berkeley, CA and Oxford: University of California Press, 1993), x; *Renaissance Self-Fashioning: From More to Shakespeare* (1980; Chicago, IL and London: University of Chicago Press, 2005), 41. In Gallagher and Greenblatt, *Practising New Historicism*, 53–9, they do discuss 'Annales-school histories of the *longue durée*', but not Braudel by name. Braudel is also cited throughout Steven Mullaney, *The Place of the Stage: License, Play, and Power in Renaissance England* (1988; Ann Arbor, MI: University of Michigan Press, 2003), which is perhaps the most fully articulated development of 'geo-history' in new historicism; Jonathan Goldberg, *James I and the Politics of Literature: Jonson, Shakespeare, Donne, and their Contemporaries* (1983; Stanford, CA: Stanford University

Press, 1989), acknowledges the *Annales* school fleetingly in a footnote, 259n.

16 For my account of Williams and his influence on cultural materialism, see 'Cultural Materialism', in *The Edinburgh Companion to Critical Theory*, ed. Stuart Sim (Edinburgh: Edinburgh University Press, 2016), 363–82.

17 Greenblatt is certainly aware of Elton's work, see *Renaissance Self-Fashioning*, 66, 262n.

18 G. R. Elton, *The Practice of History*, 2nd edn (1967; Oxford: Blackwell, 1992), vii.

19 Ibid., 206n.

20 G. R. Elton, *Return to Essentials: Some Reflections on the Present State of Historical Study* (1991; Cambridge: Cambridge University Press, 2002), 3.

21 Ibid., 11, 16, 4.

22 Ibid., 10, 12–13, 27, 41.

23 Ibid., 9.

24 Elton, *The Practice of History*, 15.

25 See G. R. Elton, *The Tudor Revolution in Government: Administrative Changes in the Reign of Henry VIII* (Cambridge: Cambridge University Press, 1953). This is the book for which Elton was most famous and in which he makes forcefully the argument that Cromwell was the man chiefly responsible for centralizing the state during the reign of Henry VIII and sowing the seeds for modern government.

26 Elton, *The Practice of History*, 9–10.

27 See Lawrence Stone, 'History and Post-Modernism', *Past & Present* 131 (May 1991): 217–18. This brief note, in which Stone feared that the new historicist view history and culture as being textual represented a 'threat' to the discipline sparked a rather massive debate in the pages of the *Past & Present* journal which raged over the next couple of years.

28 Fernand Braudel, *Civilization and Capitalism*, 3 Vols (*The Structures of Everyday Life*, *The Wheels of Commerce*, *The Perspective of the World*), trans. Siân Reynolds (New York and London: William Collins Sons & Co., 1981–92), *The Structures of Everyday Life*, 29.

29 Fernand Braudel, *The Mediterranean and the Mediterranean World in the Age of Philip II*, 2 Vols, trans. Siân Reynolds (London: William Collins Sons & Co., 1972–3), Vol. 1, 20.

30 'Lucien himself planned to write *Western Thought and Belief, 1400–1800* as a companion piece [to *Civilisation and Capitalism*] that was to accompany and complete my own book. Unfortunately, his book will never be published. My own work has thus been irrevocably deprived of this extra dimension.' Fernand Braudel, *Afterthoughts on Material Civilization and Capitalism*, trans. Patricia M. Ranum (Baltimore, MD and London: John Hopkins University Press, 1977), 3.

31 Braudel, *The Structures of Everyday Life*, 27.

32 Dan Stanislawski, 'Review of *The Mediterranean and the Mediterranean World in the Age of Philip II* by Fernand Braudel', *American Geographical Society* 64 (4) (October 1974): 597.

33 Braudel, *The Structures of Everyday Life*, 29.

34 See ibid., 203–7.

35 Ibid., 560.

36 Gallagher and Greenblatt, *Practising New Historicism*, 67.

37 Ibid., 31.

38 Quoted in Colin Jones and Roy Porter, 'Introduction', in *Reassessing Foucault: Power, Medicine, and The Body* (New York and London: Routledge, 1994), 7–8, where one can also find an excellent account of the extent and limits of Braudel's and the Annalists' influence on Foucault.

39 Colin Koopman, *Genealogy as Critique: Foucault and the Problems of Modernity* (Bloomington, IN: University of Indiana Press, 2013), 132.

40 Braudel, *The Mediterranean*, Vol. 1, 19.

41 Ibid., Vol. 2, 1243–4.

42 Michael Foucault, *The Order of Things: Archaeology of the Human Sciences* (1966; London: Routledge, 2002a), 387.

43 Gary Gutting, *Michael Foucault's Archaeology of Scientific Reason* (Cambridge: Cambridge University Press, 1989), 248–9.

44 Michel Foucault, *The Archaeology of Knowledge* (1969; London: Routledge, 2002b), 17–18.

45 Foucault, *The Order of Things*, xxi.

46 See E. M. W. Tillyard, *The Elizabethan World Picture* (1942; London: Vintage, 1959).

47 Foucault, *The Order of Things*, 251, 262.

48 Foucault, *The Archaeology of Knowledge*, 146, 120.

49 This theory has been very well disseminated and I will not outline it again here. For my own account see *Shakespeare and Contemporary Theory*, 78–96. I will also revisit it in Chapter 3.

50 Gallagher and Greenblatt, *Practising New Historicism*, 70–2, 74, 52, 16.

51 Graham Bradshaw, *Misrepresentations: Shakespeare and the Materialists* (Ithaca, NY: Cornell University Press, 1993), 81–2.

52 See Richard T. Vann, 'The Reception of Hayden White', *History and Theory* 37 (2) (May 1998): 143–61.

53 Hayden White, 'The Burden of History', *History and Theory* 5 (2) (1966): 127.

54 Jameson, *Postmodernism*, 17.

55 Gallagher and Greenblatt, *Practising New Historicism*, 67, 51.

56 Louis A. Montrose, 'Professing the Renaissance: The Poetics and Politics of Culture', in *The New Historicism*, ed. H. Aram Veeser (New York and London: Routledge, 1989), 23.

57 Louis A. Montrose, *The Purpose of Playing: Shakespeare and the Cultural Politics of the Elizabethan Theater* (Chicago, IL: University of Chicago Press, 1996), 16.

58 Harold Aram Veeser, 'Review of *The New Historicism and Other Old-Fashioned Topics* by Brook Thomas', *Modern Philology* 91 (3) (February 1994b): 404.

59 See Brian Vickers, *Appropriating Shakespeare: Contemporary Critical Quarrels* (New Haven, CT: Yale University Press, 1993), 214–71.

60 Howard Felperin, *The Uses of the Canon: Elizabethan Literature and Contemporary Theory* (Oxford: Clarendon Press, 1990), ix.

61 Gallagher and Greenblatt, *Practising New Historicism*, 20.

62 Ibid., 21.

63 Clifford Geertz, *The Interpretation of Cultures: Sketched Essays* (New York: Basic Books, 1973), 452.

64 Gallagher and Greenblatt, *Practising New Historicism*, 27. For a fuller articulation of this view, see Parvini, *Shakespeare and Contemporary Theory*, 50–2.

65 Gallagher and Greenblatt, *Practising New Historicism*, 26.

66 Geertz, *The Interpretation of Cultures*, 10–11.

67 Alun Munslow, *Deconstructing History*, 2nd edn (1997; New York and London: Routledge, 2006), 34.

68 On the reluctance of the Braudel and the Annalists to accept the view of history-as-narrative see Linda Orr, 'The Revenge of Literature: A History of History', *New Literary History* 18 (1) (Autumn 1986): 5.

69 See, for example, Sonja Laden, 'Recuperating the Archive: Anecdotal Evidence and Questions of "Historical Realism"', *Poetics Today* 25 (1) (Spring 2004): 1–24; Theodora Papadopoulou, 'Circulating through "Languages and Tales": Stephen Greenblatt's *Cardenio*', in *Reinventing the Renaissance*, ed. Sarah Annes Brown, Robert I. Lublin and Lynsey McCulloch (New York and London: Palgrave Macmillan, 2013), 77–91; and Pilar Hidalgo, *Paradigms Found: Feminist, Gay and New Historicist Readings of Shakespeare* (Amsterdam: Rodopi, 2001), 71–82. The most penetrating and fascinating study of the consequences of the new historicist anti-disciplinary style can be found in Susan Peck *in the Humanities and Sciences* (Carbondale, IL: Southern Illinois University Press, 1994), 109–46.

70 Jameson, *Postmodernism*, 187.

71 Veeser, 'Introduction, in *The New Historicism Reader*, 7.

Chapter 2

1 Lisa Hopkins, *Beginning Shakespeare* (Manchester: Manchester University Press, 2005), 63.

2 Graham Bradshaw, *Misrepresentations: Shakespeare and the Materialists* (Ithaca, NY: Cornell University Press, 1993), 6.

3 See Robin Headlam Wells, 'The Fortunes of Tillyard', *English Studies* 65 (5) (1985): 391–443.

4 Robin Headlam Wells, *Shakespeare's Politics: A Contextual Introduction* (New York and London: Continuum, 2009), 189–90.

5 Vickers, *Appropriating Shakespeare*, 216.

6 J. W. Lever, 'Shakespeare and the Ideas of his Time', *Shakespeare Survey* 29 (1976): 85; Michael Taylor, *Shakespeare: Criticism in the Twentieth Century* (Oxford: Oxford University Press, 2001), 168.

7 Taylor, *Shakespeare: Criticism in the Twentieth Century*, 168–9, 182; Lever, 'Shakespeare and the Ideas of his Time', 84. Note that it would not be fair to say that the new historicist neglect of these critics has been total, in fact one will find citations to all of them in many new historicist studies. I think the bigger issue has been the way in which new historicism has been reported and contextualized (i.e. as being responsible for the overthrow of Tillyard and bringing about an end to the dominance of formalism). It is this, rather than the question of whether or not these older critics have been read by its practitioners, that is at stake.

8 Wells, *Shakespeare's Politics*, 190–1. For a reiteration of largely the same argument, see also 'Historicism and "Presentism" in Early Modern Studies', *The Cambridge Quarterly* 29 (1) (2000): 37–60. It is also worth noting that Wells is not entirely fair to all these critics; Hugh Grady, for example, is careful to point out that Tillyard is not representative of all 'old historicist' scholarship, in *The Modernist Shakespeare: Critical Texts in a Material Word* (Oxford: Clarendon Press, 1991), 160 n.8.

9 Note that in contextualizing new historicism as being a

specifically Shakespearean phenomenon in origin, I am adopting a position that some might find contentious. See, for example, Brook Thomas, *The New Historicism and Other Old-Fashioned Topics* (Princeton, NJ: Princeton University Press, 1991), which is a study that I admittedly find very peculiar and singular in its focus. Thomas professes to locate new historicism in a wider American literary tradition: 'The Pragmatic Revolt in American history' (81). It contains no references to any of the critics I discuss in this chapter before Greenblatt (not even Stephen Orgel), or even 'old' historicists such as E. M. W. Tillyard or Lily B. Campbell. It is clear from his account that Thomas is not a Shakespearean, and, in that, his study differs sharply from my own. This is remarkable, because it has ostensibly similar aims to this one and yet casts itself into a completely different intellectual milieu. I think Thomas's study functions far better as a potted history of the American academy than it does of new historicism – although I suppose it is fitting for a new historicist's history of new historicism to appear mind-bendingly arbitrary to an outsider! Another book that ranges beyond Shakespeare studies is Jeremy Hawthorn, *Cunning Passages: New Historicism, Cultural Materialism and Marxism in the Contemporary Literary Debate* (New York and London: Arnold, 1996), which contains some valuable insights into new historicism as theory.

10 I will not be considering directly Tillyard's 'old' historicist contemporaries, such as Campbell, M. M. Reese, or the sometimes admired because less crude Theodore Spencer. Lever, 'Shakespeare and the Ideas of his Time', provides an excellent account of their strengths and shortcomings, esp. 79–86.

11 Douglas Bruster, *Quoting Shakespeare: Form and Culture in Early Modern Drama* (Lincoln, NE: University of Nebraska Press, 2000), 31.

12 Ann Baynes Coiro and Thomas Fulton, 'Introduction: Old, New, Now', in *Rethinking Historicism from Shakespeare to Milton*, eds Ann Baynes Coiro and Thomas Fulton (Cambridge, Cambridge University Press, 2012), 5.

13 For 'truly' formalist works see: G. Wilson Knight, *The Wheel of Fire: Interpretations of Shakespearean Tragedy* (1930; New York and London: Routledge, 2002); Caroline Spurgeon,

Shakespeare's Imagery and What It Tells Us (1935; Cambridge: Cambridge University Press, 1979); Cleanth Brooks, *The Well Wrought Urn: Studies in the Structure of Poetry* (New York: Harcourt Brace, 1947); B. Ifor Evans, *The Language of Shakespeare's Plays* (1952; New York and London: Routledge, 2005); M. M. Mahood, *Shakespeare's Wordplay* (London: Methuen, 1957); Frank Kermode, *The Patience of Shakespeare* (New York: Harcourt Brace, 1964); James L. Calderwood, *Shakespearean Metadrama* (Minneapolis, MN: University of Minnesota Press, 1971). For examples of works that mingle close reading with historical scholarship see: A. P. Rossiter, *Angel with Horns: Fifteen Lectures on* Shakespeare (1961; New York and Harlow: Longman, 1989); Norman Rabkin, *Shakespeare and the Common Understanding* (New York: The Free Press, 1967); William Empson, *Essays on Shakespeare*, ed. David B. Pirie (Cambridge: Cambridge University Press, 1986). For my own consideration of Rossiter, in particular, see *Shakespeare and Contemporary Theory: New Historicism and Cultural Materialism* (New York and London: Bloomsbury, 2012), 18–19 and *Shakespeare's History Plays: Rethinking Historicism* (Edinburgh: Edinburgh University Press, 2012), 177, 193.

14 Jürgen Pieters, *Moments of Negotiation: The New Historicism of Stephen Greenblatt* (Amsterdam: Amsterdam University Press, 2001), 26.

15 G. K. Hunter, 'Review of *Shakespeare's Festive Comedy: A Study of Dramatic Form and Its Relation to Social Custom* by C. L. Barber', *The Review of English Studies* 12 (45) (February 1961): 78.

16 Dover Wilson was Greenblatt's own choice for chief representative of the 'old' historicism; see Stephen Greenblatt, 'Introduction', in *The Power of Forms*, ed. Stephen Greenblatt (Norman, OK: Pilgrim Books, 1982), 5–6. Yet we might take *What Happens in Hamlet?*, 3rd edn (1935; Cambridge: Cambridge University Press, 1986) as a paradigmatic instance of New Criticism in practice. Incidentally, his later work, *The Fortunes of Falstaff* (1943; Cambridge: Cambridge University Press, 1970), is more broadly 'old' historicist, but still contains many passages of close reading in the manner of the earlier book.

17 L. C. Knights, *Drama and Society in the Age of Jonson* (London: Chatto and Windus, 1937).

18 I should mention here two influential studies, Robert Weimann, *Shakespeare and the Popular Tradition in the Theatre: Studies in the Social Dimension of Dramatic Form and Function*, ed. Robert Schwartz (1978; Baltimore, MD: John Hopkins University Press, 1987) and David Bevington, *Tudor Drama and Politics: A Critical Approach to Topical Meaning* (Cambridge, MA: Harvard University Press, 1968), that I believe belong to a tradition of materialist-historicist scholarship, separate from both new historicism and cultural materialism, that has continued through the 1980s and 1990s to today, and it perhaps at some point quietly took over new historicism as the most dominant approach in Shakespeare studies. I will return to this in Chapter 7.

19 I am indebted in this chapter to two books by Hugh Grady, *The Modernist Shakespeare*, esp. 77–191, and *Shakespeare's Universal Wolf: Studies in Early Modern Reification* (Oxford: Clarendon Press, 1996), esp. 1–25. Both books have an acute sense of the intelligence and importance of this pre-1980s scholarship and provide superb overviews of the broader intellectual traditions at play in the main critical schools.

20 Friedrich Engels, *The Origin of the Family, Private Property and the State* (1894; New York and London: Penguin, 2010); James George Frazer, *The Golden Bough: A Study in Magic and Religion*, ed. Robert Fraser (1890–1922; abr. Oxford: Oxford University Press, 1994); Edward Westermarck, *The History of Human Marriage*, 3 Vols (London: Macmillan, 1891); Edward Westermarck, *The Origin and Development of Moral Ideas*, 2 Vols (London: Macmillan, 1906).

21 Robert Ackerman, *J. G. Frazer: His Life and Work* (Cambridge: Cambridge University Press, 1987), 3.

22 Bronisław Malinowski, *A Scientific Theory of Culture and Other Essays* (1944; New York and London: Routledge, 2002), 176.

23 See James E. Miller Jr., *T. S. Eliot: The Making of an American Poet: 1888–1922* (University Park, PA: University of Pennsylvania Press, 2005), 346; and for an extended consideration of Frazer's influence on Eliot: Manju Jain, *T. S. Eliot and American Philosophy: The Harvard Years* (Cambridge: Cambridge University Press, 1992), 117–32.

24 Sigmund Freud, *Totem and Taboo: Resemblances Between the Mental Lives of Savages and Neurotics* (1913; Greentop, MO: Greentop Academic Press, 2011); Stephen Pinker, *The Blank Slate: The Modern Denial of Human Nature* (New York and London: Penguin, 2002); Jonathan Haidt, *The Righteous Mind: Why Good People are Divided by Politics and Religion* (New York and London: Penguin, 2012).

25 Frazer, *The Golden Bough*, 494.

26 Robert Fraser, 'Introduction', in Frazer, *The Golden Bough*, xxvii.

27 See André Burguière, *The Annales School: An Intellectual History*, trans. Jane Marie Todd (Ithaca, NY: Cornell University Press, 2009), 31, 56, 74.

28 For a detailed and nuanced account of the extent of Frazer's influence on this school, see Robert Ackerman, *The Myth and Ritual School: J. G. Frazer and the Cambridge Ritualists* (New York and London: Routledge, 2002). See also Stanley Edgar Hyman, 'The Ritual View of Myth and the Mythic', *The Journal of American Folklore* 68 (270), 'Myth: A Symposium' (October–December 1955); 462–72; and for discussion of Fergusson in particular, Haskell M. Block, 'Cultural Anthropology and Contemporary Literary Criticism', *The Journal of Aesthetics and Art Criticism* 11 (1) (September 1952): 46–54. For a fine overview up until the end of the 1950s, see Robert Hapgood, 'Shakespeare and the Ritualists', *Shakespeare Survey* 15 (1962): 111–24. For a book- length collection, as it pertains to literary theory, see Robert A. Segal, *The Myth and Ritual Theory: An Anthology* (Oxford: Blackwell, 1998), and, especially as it pertains to Shakespeare, Herbert Weisinger,'The Myth and Ritual Approach to Shakespearean Tragedy', in that volume, 267–84.

29 Stanley Edgar Hyman, *The Tangled Bank: Darwin, Marx, Frazer and Freud as Imaginative Writers* (New York: Atheneum, 1962), 439.

30 Patricia Waugh, *Literary Theory and Criticism: An Oxford*

Guide (Oxford: Oxford University Press, 2006), 123; Oscar James Campbell, ed., *A Shakespeare Encyclopaedia* (1966; London: Methuen, 1974), 578–9.

31 See Maud Bodkin, *The Archetypal Patterns of Poetry* (1934; Oxford: Oxford University Press, 1965); and Northrop Frye, *The Anatomy of Criticism: Four Essays* (1957; Princeton, NJ: Princeton University Press, 2000).

32 Northrop Frye, *A Natural Perspective: The Development of Shakespearean Comedy and Romance* (New York: University of Columbia Press, 1965), 58.

33 Francis Fergusson, *The Idea of Theater: A Study of Ten Plays, The Art of Drama in Changing Perspective* (1949; Princeton, NJ: Princeton University Press, 1968), 12, 14. Reference to Harrison in a footnote, 26n.

34 Francis Fergusson, *Shakespeare: The Pattern in His Carpet* (New York: Delacorte Press, 1970).

35 See Ernest Jones, *Hamlet and Oedipus: A Study into Classic Psychoanalytic Interpretation* (1949; W. W. Norton, 1976).

36 Fergusson, *The Idea of Theater*, 112–13.

37 Ibid., 120, 116.

38 See Arthur O. Lovejoy, *The Great Chain of Being: A Study of the History of an Idea* (1936; Cambridge, MA: University of Harvard Press, 1976).

39 Fergusson, *The Idea of Theater*, 116–17.

40 See Peter Erickson and Coppélia Kahn, eds, *Shakespeare's 'Rough Magic': Renaissance Essays in Honor of C. L. Barber* (Newark, NJ: University of Delaware Press, 1985).

41 C. L. Barber, *Shakespeare's Festive Comedy: A Study of Dramatic Form and Its Relation to Social Custom* (1959; Princeton, NJ: Princeton University Press, 2012), 10n. For references to Frazer, see 140, 190, 235.

42 Stephen Greenblatt, 'Foreword', in Barber, *Shakespeare's Festive Comedy*, xiv. For Hunter's complaint, see Hunter, 'Review of *Shakespeare's Festive Comedy*', 80.

43 Barber, *Shakespeare's Festive Comedy*, 238.

44 Ibid., 220–1.

45 For an excellent overview of Barber's politics and intellectual development, see Peter Erickson, 'C. L. Barber', in *Empson, Wilson Knight, Barber, Kott: Great Shakespeareans:, Volume XIII*, ed. Hugh Grady (New York and London: Bloomsbury, 2012), 91–127.

46 Barber, *Shakespeare's Festive Comedy*, 251.

47 Ibid., 7, 250.

48 Ibid., 278–9.

49 Stephen Greenblatt, *Shakespearean Negotiations: The Circulation of Social Energy in Renaissance England* (Berkeley, CA: University of California Press, 1988), 72.

50 Ibid., 52–5.

51 Barber, *Shakespeare's Festive Comedy*, 246.

52 See E. M. W. Tillyard, *Shakespeare's History Plays* (1944; New York and London: Penguin, 1991); Lily B. Campbell, *Shakespeare's 'Histories': Mirrors of Elizabethan Policy* (1947; New York and London: Routledge, 2005); M. M. Reese, *The Cease of Majesty: A Study of Shakespeare's History Plays* (New York: St. Martin's Press, 1961).

53 Lever, 'Shakespeare and the Ideas of his Time', 89.

54 Nonetheless, Lever himself was still fighting that battle three years after Sanders and performed his own dismantling of Tillyard in J. W. Lever, *The Tragedy of State* (London: Methuen, 1971), esp. 5–7.

55 I am broadly persuaded of this view of Shakespeare myself, see *Shakespeare's History Plays*, 173–94.

56 Wilbur Sanders, *The Dramatist and the Received Idea: Studies in the Plays of Marlowe and Shakespeare* (Cambridge: Cambridge University Press, 1968), 92, 59, 142, 242.

57 Ibid., 145, 149.

58 See Raymond Williams, *Marxism and Literature* (Oxford: Oxford University Press, 1977), 121–4.

59 Stephen Orgel and Roy C. Strong, *Inigo Jones: Theatre of the Stuart Court*, 2 Vols (London: Sotheby Parke Bernet, 1973).

60 Stephen Orgel, *The Illusion of Power: Political Theater in the*

English Renaissance (Berkeley, CA: University of California Press, 1975), 42–3, 16, 14.

61 Richard Wilson, 'Introduction: Historicising New Historicism', in *New Historicism and Renaissance Drama* (New York and London: Longman, 1992), 10.

62 Orgel, *The Illusion of Power*, 51, 81.

63 Claire Colebrook, *New Literary Histories: New Historicism and Contemporary Criticism* (Manchester: Manchester University Press, 1997), 199–200.

64 Jean E. Howard, 'The New Historicism in Renaissance Studies', *English Literary Renaissance* 16 (1) (December 1986): 18; Louis A. Montrose, 'Renaissance Literary Studies and the Subject of History', *English Literary Renaissance* 16 (1) (December 1986): 7–8.

Chapter 3

1 Stephen Greenblatt, *Shakespearean Negotiations: The Circulation of Social Energy in Renaissance England* (Berkeley, CA: University of California Press, 1988), 6–7.

2 Jean E. Howard, 'The New Historicism in Renaissance Studies', *English Literary Renaissance* 16 (1) (December, 1986): 18.

3 Richard C. McCoy, 'Lord of Liberty: Francis Davison and the Cult of Elizabeth', in *The Reign of Elizabeth I: Court and Culture in the Last Decade*, ed. John Guy (Cambridge: Cambridge University Press, 1995), 213.

4 Blair Worden, 'Tolerant Repression', *London Review of Books* 12 (9) (May 1990): 17.

5 See Jean E. Howard, 'Old Wine, New Bottles', *Shakespeare Quarterly* 35 (2) (Summer 1984): 234–7.

6 David Scott Kastan, *Shakespeare After Theory* (New York and London: Routledge, 1999), 24.

7 Louis A. Montrose, *The Purpose of Playing: Shakespeare and the Cultural Politics of the Elizabethan Theater* (Chicago, IL: University of Chicago Press, 1996), 8.

8 For my full critique of this book see *Shakespeare's History Plays: Rethinking Historicism* (Edinburgh: Edinburgh University Press, 2012), 13–19.

9 Jonathan Goldberg, *James I and the Politics of Literature: Jonson, Shakespeare, Donne, and their Contemporaries* (1983; Stanford, CA: Stanford University Press, 1989), 8, 33.

10 See ibid., 177.

11 Leonard Tennenhouse, *Power on Display: The Politics of Shakespeare's Genres* (1986; New York and London: Routledge, 2010), 13.

12 Ibid., 128–9.

13 See for example, Peter Erickson, 'Review of *Power on Display: The Politics of Shakespeare's Genres* by Leonard Tennenhouse', *Shakespeare Quarterly* 39 (4) (Winter 1988); 'Tennenhouse hits the nail on the head too hard, driving out any possibility of complexity', 510.

14 Edward Pechter, 'The New Historicism and Its Discontents: Politicizing Renaissance Drama', *PMLA* 102 (3) (May 1987): 292–303; Graham Bradshaw, *Misrepresentations: Shakespeare and the Materialists* (Ithaca, NY: Cornell University Press, 1993); Richard Levin, in a slew of essays, including: 'Unthinkable Thoughts in the New Historicizing of English Renaissance Drama', *New Literary* History 21 (3) (Spring 1990): 433–47, '(Re)Thinking Unthinkable Thoughts', *New Literary* History 28 (3) (Summer 1997): 525–37, 'The Cultural Materialist Attack on Artistic Unity, and the Problem of Ideological Criticism', in *Ideological Approaches to Shakespeare*, eds R. P. Merrix and N. Ranson (Lewiston, NY: Edwin Mellen Press, 1992), 9–56 and 'The Old and the New Materialising of Shakespeare', in *The Shakespearean International Yearbook, Vol. 1: Where Are We Now in Shakespearean Studies?*, eds W. R. Elton and John M. Mucciolo (Brookfield, VT and Aldershot: Ashgate, 1999), 87–107 – all these are usefully collected in his appropriately titled collection *Looking for An Argument: Critical Encounters with the New Approaches to the Criticism of Shakespeare and his Contemporaries* (Madison, NJ: Fairleigh Dickinson University Press, 2003); and Vickers, *Appropriating Shakespeare*, 214–71.

15 See Michel Foucault, *Discipline and Punish: The Birth of the Prison*, trans. Alan Sheridan (1977; New York and London: Penguin, 1991).

16 See Louis Althusser, 'Ideology and the Ideological State Apparatus', *Lenin and Philosophy and Other Essays*, trans. Ben Brewster (1971; New York: Monthly Review Press, 2001), 85–126.

17 Michel Foucault, *The History of Sexuality, Volume 1: The Will to Knowledge*, trans. Robert Hurley (1978; New York and London: Penguin, 1998), 93.

18 Ibid., 95–6.

19 See Thomas Hobbes, *Leviathan*, ed. J. C. A. Gaskin (1651; Oxford: Oxford University Press, 2008).

20 See Louis Althusser, *For Marx*, trans. Ben Brewster (1969; New York and London, Verso: 2005), 87–128.

21 Foucault, *The History of Sexuality*, 94.

22 Ibid., 96.

23 Ibid., 97.

24 Stephen Greenblatt, *Renaissance Self-Fashioning: From More to Shakespeare* (1980; Chicago, IL and London: University of Chicago Press, 2005), 256.

25 Greenblatt, *Shakespearean Negotiations*, 2.

26 Ibid., 19.

27 See ibid., 10–12.

28 Howard Felperin, *The Uses of the Canon: Elizabethan Literature and Contemporary Theory* (Oxford: Clarendon Press, 1990), 152.

29 Greenblatt, *Shakespearean Negotiations*, 20.

30 See Stephen Greenblatt, 'Towards a Poetics of Culture', *Learning to Curse: Essays in Early Modern Culture* (1990; New York and London: Routledge, 2007), 196–215, esp. 203–4.

31 Harold Aram Veeser, 'The New Historicism', in *The New Historicism Reader* ed. Harold Aram Veeser (New York and London: Routledge, 1994), 19.

32 Greenblatt, *Shakespearean Negotiations*, 203.

33 David Foster Wallace, 'Authority and American Usage', in *Consider the Lobster and Other Essays* (New York: Little Brown and Co. 2005), 103.

34 Louis Montrose, 'New Historicisms', in *Redrawing the Boundaries: The Transformation of English and American Literary Studies*, eds Stephen Greenblatt and Giles Gunn (New York: The Modern Language Association of America, 1992), 404, 402.

35 I will return to the terms of this binary in Chapter 6, but it is worth noting that its perpetuation was partly the result of cultural materialism's attempts to define itself against new historicism. See especially Jonathan Dollimore, 'Critical Developments: Cultural Materialism, Feminism and Gender Critique, and New Historicism', in *Shakespeare: A Bibliographical Guide*, ed. Stanley Wells (Oxford: Clarendon Press, 1990), 405–28.

36 Anthony Giddens, *Central Problems in Social Theory: Action, Structure, and Contradiction in Social Analysis* (Berkeley, CA: University of California Press, 1979), 69, 71.

37 Pierre Bourdieu, *Outline of a Theory of Practice*, trans. Richard Nice (Cambridge: Cambridge University Press, 1977), 72.

38 Ibid., 79.

39 Ibid., 87.

40 Marshall Sahlins, *Islands of History* (Chicago, IL: University of Chicago Press, 1985), vii, xiv.

41 Montrose, *The Purpose of Playing*, 15.

42 Ibid., 75.

43 G. R. Elton, *England Under the Tudors*, 3rd edn (1955; New York and London: Routledge, 2015) 469, 473.

44 Frank Lentricchia, 'Foucault's Legacy: A New Historicism?', in *The New Historicism*, ed. Harold Aram Veeser (New York and London: Routledge, 1989), 238.

45 Stanley Fish, 'Commentary: The Young and the Restless', in *The New Historicism*, ed. Harold Aram Veeser (New York and London: Routledge, 1989), 307.

46 For a full consideration of new historicism's impact on the

notion of 'character' in Shakespeare's plays see Neema Parvini, *Shakespeare and Cognition: Thinking Fast and Slow Through Character* (New York and London: Palgrave Macmillan, 2015), esp. 1–11.

Chapter 4

1 T. F. Wharton, *Measure for Measure: The Critics Debate* (London: Macmillan, 1989), 9.

2 Michael Jamieson, 'The Problem Plays, 1920–1970: A Retrospect', *Shakespeare Studies* 25 (1972): 4. For an excellent overview of the critical history of *Measure for Measure*, see George L. Geckle, 'Introduction, in *Measure for Measure. Shakespeare: The Critical Tradition*, ed. George L. Geckle (New York and London: The Athlone Press, 2001), 1–76; see also Bruce T. Sajdek, *Shakespeare Index: An Annotated Bibliography of Critical Articles on the Plays 1959–1983*, 2 Vols (Millwood, NY: Kraus International Publications, 1992), Vol. 1, 509–28 – this is a truly invaluable volume for criticism from the 1960s and 1970s.

3 Quoted in E. K. Chambers, *William Shakespeare: A Study of Facts and Problems*, 2 Vols (Oxford: Oxford University Press, 1930), Vol. 2, 331.

4 Leah S. Marcus, *Puzzling Shakespeare: Local Reading and Its Discontents* (Berkeley, CA: University of California Press, 1988), 163. The materials are usefully collected in James I, *The True Law of Free Monarchies; And, Basilikon Doron*, eds Daniel Fisclin and Mark Fortier (Toronto, ON: CRRS Publications, 1996).

5 See Frederick George Marcham, 'James I of England and the Little Beagle Letters', in *Persecution and Liberty: Essays in Honor of George Lincoln Burr* (New York: Century Company, 1931), 311–34.

6 James I, *The True Law of Free Monarchies; And, Basilikon Doron*, 89.

7 See David Stevenson, '"The Gudeman of Ballangeich":

Rambles in the Afterlife of James V', *Folklore* 115 (2) (August 2004): 187–200.

8 Francis Fergusson, *Shakespeare: The Pattern in His Carpet* (New York: Delacorte Press, 1970).

9 See Sajdek, *Shakespeare Index*, 509–28, which lists dozens of pro-Duke readings and just as many on the anti-Duke side.

10 Levin was not as forthcoming in naming his targets in 1979 as he would be later, and does not name his sources, but one imagines he is referring to Josephine Waters Bennett, *Measure for Measure as Royal Entertainment* (New York: Columbia University Press, 1966), and Roy Battenhouse, '*Measure for Measure* and King James', *CLIO* 7 (1978): 193–215, especially as Levin was to feud with Battenhouse in the pages of *CLIO* for the duration of that year. See also Darryl J. Gless, *Measure for Measure, the Law and the Convent* (Princeton. NJ: Princeton University Press, 1979), esp. 154–9 – though this might have appeared too late for Levin reasonably to have been expected to have read it by the time of his own book's printing.

11 Richard Levin, *New Readings vs. Old Plays: Recent Trends in the Reinterpretation of Renaissance Drama* (Chicago, IL: University of Chicago Press, 1979), 171–93, and on 'Fluellenism', 209–29

12 Kevin A. Quarmby, 'Narrative of Negativity: Whig Historiography and the Spectre of King James in *Measure for Measure*', in *Shakespeare Survey 64: Shakespeare as Cultural Catalyst*, ed. Peter Holland (Cambridge: Cambridge University Press, 2011), 306; 300–16.

13 Ivo Kamps and Karen Ribner, *Measure for Measure: Texts and Contexts* (Boston, MA: St. Martin's, 2004), 125.

14 Marcus, *Puzzling Shakespeare*, 38.

15 A. D. Nuttall, *A New Mimeses: Shakespeare and the Representation of Reality*, 2nd edn (1983; New Haven, CT: Yale University Press, 2007), vii–viii.

16 For an engaging discussion of this, see Albert H. Tricomi, *Reading Tudor-Stuart Texts through Cultural Historicism* (Gainesville, FL: University Press of Florida, 1996), 1–17 – this is an under-read study, which contains valuable insights into new historicist theory and practice. His critique raises several salient points to which we will return in Chapter 6.

17 Jonathan Goldberg, *James I and the Politics of Literature: Jonson, Shakespeare, Donne, and their Contemporaries* (1983; Stanford, CA: Stanford University Press, 1989), 232.

18 Clifford Geertz, *The Interpretation of Cultures: Sketched Essays* (New York: Basic Books, 1973), 448–52. For my own fuller critique of this see *Shakespeare and Contemporary Theory: New Historicism and Cultural Materialism* (New York and London: Bloomsbury, 2012), 47–55.

19 Goldberg, *James I and the Politics of Literature*, 236–7.

20 Ibid., 239.

21 Leonard Tennenhouse, *Power on Display: The Politics of Shakespeare's Genres* (1986; New York and London: Routledge, 2010), 155–9.

22 See ibid., 76–81.

23 Stephen Greenblatt, *Shakespearean Negotiations: The Circulation of Social Energy in Renaissance England* (Berkeley, CA: University of California Press, 1988), 136–42.

24 Steven Mullaney, *The Place of the Stage: License, Play, and Power in Renaissance England* (1988; Ann Arbor, MI: University of Michigan Press, 2003), 105–11.

25 Cedric Watts, *William Shakespeare: Measure for Measure* (New York and London: Penguin, 1986), 102.

26 Andrew Barnaby and Joan Wry, 'Authorized Versions: *Measure for Measure* and the Politics of Biblical Translation', *Renaissance Quarterly* 51 (1998): 1225n.

27 Marcus, *Puzzling Shakespeare*, 164–84.

28 Ibid., 184–202.

29 Craig A. Bernthal, 'Staging Justice: James I and the Trial Scenes of *Measure for Measure*', *Studies in English Literature, 1500–1900* 32 (2) (Spring 1992): 256.

30 Ibid., 263.

31 Ibid., 264.

32 See, for example, the readings by David McCandless, Arthur L.

Little Jr and Robert N. Watson, in *Shakespearean Power and Punishment: A Volume of Essays*, ed. Gillian Murray Kendall (Teaneck, NJ: Fairleigh Dickinson University Press, 1998), 89–158 – which might be seen as a broadly new historicist collection; see also the aforementioned essays: Barnaby and Wry, 'Authorized Versions', and Quarmby, 'Narrative of Negativity'.

33 Brian Vickers, 'General Editor's Preface', in *Measure for Measure. Shakespeare: The Critical Tradition*, ed. George L. Geckle (New York and London: The Athlone Press, 2001), xxx.

Chapter 5

1 Jean E. Howard, 'Feminism and the Question of History: Resituating the Debate', *Women's Studies: An Interdisciplinary Journal* 19 (2) (1991): 149.

2 David Bevington, 'Two Households, Both Alike in Dignity: The Uneasy Alliance between New Historicists and Feminists', *English Literary Renaissance* 25 (3) (September 1995): 307–19.

3 Kathleen McLuskie, 'The Patriarchal Bard: Feminist Criticism and Shakespeare: *King Lear* and *Measure for Measure*', in *Political Shakespeare*, eds Jonathan Dollimore and Alan Sinfield, 2nd edn (1985; Manchester: Manchester University Press, 2012), 91.

4 Both Levin's attack and the letter are reprinted in *Looking for An Argument: Critical Encounters with the New Approaches to the Criticism of Shakespeare and his Contemporaries* (Madison, NJ: Fairleigh Dickinson University Press, 2003), 29–54.

5 Stephen Greenblatt, *Learning to Curse: Essays in Early Modern Culture* (1990; New York and London: Routledge, 2007), 186, 190–1.

6 On this score, although I would share a scepticism about the assumptions of Freudian psychoanalysis, I strongly disagree with new historicism, see *Shakespeare and Cognition: Thinking*

Fast and Slow through Character (New York and London: Palgrave Macmillan, 2015), esp. 1–35.

7 See Carolyn Ruth Swift Lenz, Gayle Greene and Carol Thomas Neely, eds, *The Woman's Part: Feminist Criticism of Shakespeare* (Urbana, IL: University of Illinois Press, 1980).

8 Gayle Greene, 'The Myth of Neutrality, Again', *Shakespeare Left and Right*, ed. Ivo Kamps (New York and London: Routledge, 1991), 27.

9 Lynda Boose, 'The Family in Shakespeare Studies; or – Studies in the Family of Shakespeareans; or – The Politics of Politics', *Renaissance Quarterly* 4 (4) (Winter 1987): 714–26.

10 Greene, 'The Myth of Neutrality, Again', 28.

11 Quoted in Kamps, *Shakespeare Left and Right*, 3.

12 She is talking about Jean E. Howard and Marion F. O'Connor, eds, *Shakespeare Reproduced: The Text in History and Ideology* (New York and London: Routledge, 1987).

13 Greene, 'The Myth of Neutrality, Again', 28–9.

14 Boose, 'The Family in Shakespeare Studies, 719, 727.

15 Ibid., 727. Note, Boose appears to have the date of the meeting off by two years: it seems to have taken place in Cambridge, MA in 1984, not in Boston in 1982.

16 Ibid., 731.

17 See Jonathan Goldberg, 'Shakespearean Inscriptions: The Voicing of Power', in *Shakespeare's Hand* (Minneapolis, MN: University of Minnesota Press, 2003), 55–78.

18 Boose, 'The Family in Shakespeare Studies', 741.

19 Carol Thomas Neely, 'Constructing the Subject: Feminist Practice and the New Renaissance Discourses', *English Literary Renaissance* (December 1988): 5–8.

20 See Stephen Greenblatt, 'Shakespeare and the Exorcists', in *Shakespearean Negotiations: The Circulation of Social Energy in Renaissance England* (Berkeley, CA: University of California Press, 1988), 94–128; Jonathan Dollimore, 'Transgression and Surveillance in Measure for Measure', in *Political Shakespeare*, eds Jonathan Dollimore and Alan Sinfield, 2nd edn (1985;

Manchester: Manchester University Press, 2012), 72–87; and McLuskie, 'The Patriarchal Bard'.

21 Neely, 'Constructing the Subject', 17–18.

22 Peter Erickson, *Rewriting Shakespeare, Rewriting Ourselves* (Berkeley, CA: University of California Press, 1991), 10.

23 Valerie Wayne, 'Introduction', in *The Matter of Difference: Materialist Feminist Criticism of Shakespeare*, ed. Valerie Wayne (Hemel Hempstead: Harvester Wheatsheaf, 1991b), 1, 4–5.

24 Lisa Jardine, *Still Harping on Daughters: Women and Drama in the Age of Shakespeare* (Brighton: Harvester Press, 1983).

25 Coppélia Kahn, 'The New Historicism and Renaissance Portrayals of Women', *Shakespeare Quarterly* 35 (4) (Winter 1984); 489.

26 Linda Woodbridge, *Women and the English Renaissance: Literature and the Nature of Womankind, 1540 to 1620* (Urbana, IL: University of Illinois Press, 1984); Catherine Belsey, *The Subject of Tragedy: Identity and Difference in Renaissance Drama* (New York and London: Methuen, 1985); Dympna Callaghan, *Woman and Gender in Renaissance Tragedy: A Study of King Lear, Othello, The Duchess of Malfi and The White Devil* (Hemel Hempstead: Harvester Wheatsheaf, 1989).

27 Karen Newman, *Fashioning Femininity and English Renaissance Drama* (Chicago, IL: University of Chicago Press, 1991), 11.

28 See Phyllis Rackin, *Stages of History: Shakespeare's English Chronicles* (Ithaca, NY: Cornell University Press, 1990).

29 Jean E. Howard and Phyllis Rackin, *Engendering a Nation: A Feminist Account of Shakespeare's English Histories* (New York and London: Routledge, 1997).

30 Peter J. Smith, 'The Critical Backstory', in *Richard III: A Critical Reader*, ed. Annaliese Connolly (New York and London: Bloomsbury Arden, 2013), 45.

Chapter 6

1 Vickers, *Appropriating Shakespeare*, 215.

2 Geoffrey Galt Harpham, 'Foucault and the New Historicism', *American Literary History* 3 (2) (Summer 1991): 368.

3 Stephen Greenblatt, *Will in the World: How Shakespeare Became Shakespeare* (New York: W. W. Norton, 2005) and *The Swerve: How the World Became Modern* (New York: W. W. Norton, 2012).

4 A. D. Nuttall, *Shakespeare: The Thinker* (New Haven, CT: Yale University Press, 2007b); Marjorie B. Garber, *Shakespeare After All* (New York and London: Random House, 2004); Frank Kermode, *Shakespeare's Language* (Harmondsworth: Penguin, 2000); Harold Bloom, *Shakespeare: The Invention of the Human* (New York: Riverhead Books, 1998).

5 I mean 'right' and 'left' here as relative terms with the 'right' generally defending older traditions of scholarship from 'new' theory, while the 'left' pushes for ever-more radical and political readings, as per my usage on pages 67, 102.

6 Edward Pechter, 'The New Historicism and Its Discontents', 299.

7 Jeremy Hawthorn, *Cunning Passages: New Historicism, Cultural Materialism and Marxism in the Contemporary Literary Debate* (New York and London: Arnold, 1996), 4.

8 Howard Felperin, *The Uses of the Canon: Elizabethan Literature and Contemporary Theory* (Oxford: Clarendon Press, 1990), 142.

9 For a much fuller account of cultural materialism and its genesis, see Neema Parvini, 'Cultural Materialism', in *The Edinburgh Companion to Critical Theory*, ed. Stuart Sim (Edinburgh: Edinburgh University Press, 2016), 363–82. as well as *Shakespeare and Contemporary Theory: New Historicism and Cultural Materialism* (New York and London: Bloomsbury, 2012), esp. 122–47; and for my critique of the approach see *Shakespeare's History Plays: Rethinking Historicism* (Edinburgh: Edinburgh University Press, 2012), esp. 33–51. See also from the Arden Shakespeare and Theory

series, Christopher Marlow, *Shakespeare and Cultural Materialism* (New York and London: Bloomsbury Arden, 2017, forthcoming).

10 Jonathan Dollimore, 'Critical Developments: Cultural Materialism, Feminism and Gender Critique, and New Historicism', in *Shakespeare: A Bibliographical Guide*, ed. Stanley Wells (Oxford: Clarendon Press, 1990), 414.

11 Terence Hawkes, *Meaning By Shakespeare* (New York and London: Routledge, 1992), 8.

12 Mark Robson, *Stephen Greenblatt* (New York and London: Routledge, 2007), 27.

13 Hawkes, *Meaning By Shakespeare*, 3.

14 Scott Wilson, *Cultural Materialism: Theory and Practice* (Oxford: Blackwell, 1995), 86.

15 Felperin, *The Uses of the Canon*, 157.

16 Walter Cohen, 'Political Criticism of Shakespeare', in *Shakespeare Reproduced: The Text in History and Ideology*, eds Jean E. Howard and Marion F. O'Connor (New York and London: Routledge, 1987), 33, 34–5, 38.

17 See Parvini, *Shakespeare's History Plays*, 10–32.

18 Felperin, *The Uses of the Canon*, 154–5.

19 David Scott Kastan, *Shakespeare After Theory* (New York and London: Routledge, 1999), 29.

20 Richard Lehan, 'The Theoretical Limits of New Historicism', *New Literary History* 21 (3) (Spring 1990): 552.

21 See Cary DiPietro and Hugh Grady, eds, *Shakespeare and the Urgency of Now: Criticism and Theory in the 21st Century* (New York and London: Palgrave Macmillan, 2013).

22 Terence Hawkes, *Shakespeare in the Present* (New York and London: Routledge, 2002), 4.

23 Evelyn Gajowski, 'Beyond Historicism: Presentism, Subjectivity, Politics', *Literature Compass* 7 (8) (2010): 1.

24 Ibid., 2.

25 Hugh Grady and Terence Hawkes, 'Introduction: Presenting Presentism', in *Presentist Shakespeares*, eds Hugh Grady and

Terence Hawkes (New York and London: Routledge, 2007), 2, 4.

26 Joseph Carroll, *Reading Human Nature: Literary Darwinism in Theory and Practice* (Albany, NY: State University Press of New York, 2011), 275–6. See also Brian Boyd, *On the Origin of Stories: Evolution, Cognition, and Fiction* (Cambridge, MA and London: Harvard University Press, 2009).

27 Andy Mousley, *Re-Humanising Shakespeare: Literary Humanism, Wisdom and Modernity* (Edinburgh: Edinburgh University Press, 2007), 10. See also, Robin Headlam Wells, *Shakespeare's Humanism* (Cambridge: Cambridge University Press, 2005).

28 Nuttall, *Shakespeare: The Thinker*, 11, 24, emphasis in the original.

29 See Paul Yachnin and Jessica Slights, eds, *Shakespeare and Character: Theory, History, Performance, and Theatrical Persons* (New York and London: Palgrave Macmillan, 2009); Michael D. Bristol (ed.), *Shakespeare and Moral Agency*, (New York and London: Continuum, 2010); Neema Parvini, *Shakespeare and Cognition: Thinking Fast and Slow Through Character* (New York and London: Palgrave Macmillan, 2015).

30 See Mary Thomas Crane, *Shakespeare's Brain: Reading with Cognitive Theory* (Princeton, NJ: Princeton University Press, 2000); Amy Cook, *Shakespearean Neuroplay: Reinvigorating the Study of Dramatic Texts and Performance through Cognitive Science* (New York and London: Palgrave Macmillan, 2010); Evelyn Tribble, *Cognition in the Globe: Attention and Memory in Shakespeare's Theatre* (New York and London: Palgrave Macmillan, 2011); Raphael Lyne, *Shakespeare, Rhetoric, and Cognition* (Cambridge: Cambridge University Press, 2011); and Laurie Johnson, John Sutton and Evelyn Tribble, eds, *Embodied Cognition and Shakespeare's Theatre: The Early Modern Body-Mind* (New York and London: Routledge, 2014).

31 Graham Bradshaw, *Misrepresentations: Shakespeare and the Materialists* (Ithaca, NY: Cornell University Press, 1993), 1.

32 A. D. Nuttall, *A New Mimeses: Shakespeare and the*

Representation of Reality, 2nd edn (1983; New Haven, CT: Yale University Press, 2007a), vii.

33 Bradshaw, *Misrepresentations*, 80.

34 Richard Levin, *Looking for an Argument: Critical Encounters with the New Approaches to the Criticism of Shakespeare and his Contemporaries* (Madison, NJ: Fairleigh Dickinson University Press, 2003), 188.

35 Edward Pechter, 'The New Historicism and Its Discontents', 293. See also Bradshaw, *Misrepresentations*, 34–5; and Vickers, *Appropriating Shakespeare*, 267–71.

36 Vickers, *Appropriating Shakespeare*, 267.

37 Levin, *Looking for an Argument*, 182.

38 Vickers, *Appropriating Shakespeare*, 267.

39 Ibid., 267. See also Levin, *Looking for an Argument*, 82–103.

40 On this matter of *The Tempest* specifically, I'd recommend Meredith Anne Skura's excellent essay, 'Discourse and the Individual: The Case of Colonialism in *The Tempest*', *Shakespeare Quarterly* 40 (1) (Spring 1989): 42–69.

41 See Neema Parvini, 'The Scholars and The Critics: Shakespeare studies and theory in the 2010s', *Shakespeare* 10 (2) (Spring 2014): 12–23.

42 Harold Aram Veeser, 'Introduction', in *The New Historicism* (New York and London: Routledge, 1989), ix.

43 Frank Kermode, *The Uses of Error* (Cambridge, MA: University of Harvard Press, 1991), 125–6.

Chapter 7

1 Rebecca Munson and Claude Willan, 'The Children of New Historicism: Literary Scholarship, Professionalization, and the Will to Publish', in *The Limits of Literary Historicism*, eds Allen Dunn and Thomas F. Haddox (Knoxville, TN: University of Tennessee Press, 2012), 9.

2 Ibid., 9–10.

3 Michael L. Hays, 'Review of *Shakespeare After Theory* by David Scott Kastan', *Comparative Drama* 31 (1) (Spring 2001): 125.

4 Stephen Greenblatt, 'Introduction', in *The Power of Forms*, ed. Stephen Greenblatt (Norman, OK: Pilgrim Books, 1982), 5.

5 Ian Frederick Moulton, 'Review', *Shakespeare Quarterly* 6 (3) (Fall 2015): 374.

6 Allen Dunn and Thomas F. Haddox, 'The Enigma of Critical Distance; or, Why Historicists Need Convictions', in *The Limits of Literary Historicism*, eds Allen Dunn and Thomas F. Haddox (Knoxville, TN: University of Tennessee Press, 2012), xix. They are quoting Alan Liu, 'The Power of Formalism: The New Historicism', *English Literary History* 56 (4) (Winter 1989): 754.

7 Gordon McMullan, 'Preface: Renaissance Configurations', in *Renaissance Configurations: Voices/Bodies/Spaces*, ed. Gordon McMullan (New York and London: Macmillan, 1998), xv–xvi, emphasis mine.

8 Patricia Fumerton, 'Introduction: A New New Historicism', in *Renaissance Culture and the Everyday* (Philadelphia, PA: University of Philadelphia Press, 1999), 3; David Scott Kastan, *Shakespeare After Theory* (New York and London: Routledge, 1999), 13.

9 Fumerton, 'Introduction: A New New Historicism', 1.

10 Ibid., 3.

11 See Michel de Certeau, *The Practice of Everyday Life*, trans. Steven Rendell (Berkeley, CA: University of California Press, 1984).

12 Fumerton, 'Introduction: A New New Historicism', 4, 5.

13 Fernand Braudel, *Civilization and Capitalism*, 3 Vols (*The Structures of Everyday Life, The Wheels of Commerce, The Perspective of the World*), trans. Siân Reynolds (New York and London: William Collins Sons & Co., 1981–92), *The Structures of Everyday Life*, 27.

14 Deborah Shuger, 'The "I" of the Beholder: Renaissance Mirrors and the Reflexive Mind', in *Renaissance Culture and the*

Everyday (Philadelphia, PA: University of Philadelphia Press, 1999), 21.

15 Douglas Bruster, *Shakespeare and the Question of Culture*, 202–3.

16 Louis Althusser, 'Ideology and the Ideological State Apparatus', in *Lenin and Philosophy and Other Essays*, ed. Fredric Jameson, trans. Ben Brewster (1971; rpr. New York: Monthly Review Press, 2001), 85–126.

17 Bruster, *Shakespeare and the Question of Culture*, 204, 203.

18 See Neema Parvini, 'The Scholars and The Critics: Shakespeare studies and theory in the 2010s', *Shakespeare* 10 (2) (Spring 2014): 212–23.

19 Kastan, *Shakespeare After Theory*, 37, 13, 31.

20 Ibid., 14.

21 Ibid., 42, 40.

22 G. R. Elton, *The Practice of History*, 2nd edn (1967; Oxford: Blackwell, 1992), vii.

23 Kastan, *Shakespeare After Theory*, 41.

24 A. D. Nuttall, *Shakespeare: The Thinker* (New Haven, CT: Yale University Press, 2007), 11, emphasis in the original.

25 Howard Felperin, *The Uses of the Canon: Elizabethan Literature and Contemporary Theory* (Oxford: Clarendon Press, 1990), 168–9.

26 Hugh Grady, 'Theory "After Theory": Christopher Pye's Reading of *Othello*', *Shakespeare Quarterly* 6 (4) (Winter 2009): 453.

27 Andrew Hadfield, 'Has Historicism Come Too Far Or, Should We Return to Form?', in *Rethinking Historicism from Shakespeare to Milton*, ed. Ann Baynes Coiro and Thomas Fulton (Cambridge, Cambridge University Press, 2012), 32.

28 Kastan, *Shakespeare After Theory*, 41–2, emphasis in the original.

29 Ibid., 121.

30 See Jonathan Gil Harris, *Sick Economies: Drama, Mercantilism, and Disease in Shakespeare's England* (University of Pennsylvania Press, 2003); Jonathan Gil Harris,

Untimely Matter in the Time of Shakespeare (Philadelphia, PA: University of Pennsylvania Press, 2008); Natasha Korda, *Shakespeare's Domestic Economies: Gender and Property in Early Modern England* (Philadelphia, PA: University of Pennsylvania Press, 2002). See also Margareta De Grazia, Maureen Quilligan and Peter Stallybrass (eds), *Subject and Object in Renaissance Culture* (Cambridge: Cambridge University Press, 1996); Ann Rosalind Jones and Peter Stallybrass, *Renaissance Clothing and the Materials of Memory* (Cambridge: Cambridge University Press, 2001).

31 Bruster, *Shakespeare and the Question of Culture*, 29.

32 Peter Grav, 'Taking Stock of Shakespeare and the New Economic Criticism', *Shakespeare* 8 (1) (May 2012): 112. For an excellent overview of these developments, see David Hawkes, *Shakespeare and Economic Theory* (New York and London: Bloomsbury Arden, 2015).

33 See Margareta De Grazia and Peter Stallybrass, 'The Materiality of the Shakespearean Text', *Shakespeare Quarterly* 44 (3) (Autumn 1993): 255–83. For Edward Pechter's piece, which dismisses this interest with material texts as being practically irrelevant to the study of literature, see 'Making Love to Our Employment; Or, the Immateriality of Arguments about the Materiality of the Shakespearean Text', *Textual Practice* 11 (1) (1997): 51–97.

BIBLIOGRAPHY

Ackerman, Robert, *J. G. Frazer: His Life and Work* (Cambridge: Cambridge University Press, 1987).

Ackerman, Robert, *The Myth and Ritual School: J. G. Frazer and the Cambridge Ritualists* (New York and London: Routledge, 2002).

Althusser, Louis, 'Ideology and the Ideological State Apparatus', in *Lenin and Philosophy and Other Essays*, trans. Ben Brewster (1971; New York: Monthly Review Press, 2001).

Althusser, Louis, *For Marx*, trans. Ben Brewster (1969; New York and London, Verso: 2005).

Barber, C. L., *Shakespeare's Festive Comedy: A Study of Dramatic Form and Its Relation to Social Custom* (1959; Princeton, NJ: Princeton University Press, 2012).

Barnaby, Andrew and Joan Wry, 'Authorized Versions: *Measure for Measure* and the Politics of Biblical Translation', *Renaissance Quarterly* 51 (1998).

Battenhouse, Roy. '*Measure for Measure* and King James', *CLIO* 7 (1978).

Belsey, Catherine, *The Subject of Tragedy: Identity and Difference in Renaissance Drama* (New York and London: Methuen, 1985).

Bennett, Josephine Waters, *Measure for Measure as Royal Entertainment* (New York: Columbia University Press, 1966).

Bernthal, Craig A., 'Staging Justice: James I and the Trial Scenes of *Measure for Measure*', *Studies in English Literature, 1500–1900* 32 (2) (Spring 1992).

Bevington, David, *Tudor Drama and Politics: A Critical Approach to Topical Meaning* (Cambridge, MA: Harvard University Press, 1968).

Bevington, David, 'Two Households, Both Alike in Dignity: The Uneasy Alliance between New Historicists and Feminists', *English Literary Renaissance* 25 (3) (September 1995).

Block, Haskell M., 'Cultural Anthropology and Contemporary Literary Criticism', *The Journal of Aesthetics and Art Criticism* 11 (1) (September 1952).

Bloom, Harold, *Shakespeare: The Invention of the Human* (New York: Riverhead Books, 1998).

Bodkin, Maud, *The Archetypal Patterns of Poetry* (1934; Oxford: Oxford University Press, 1965).

Boose, Lynda, 'The Family in Shakespeare Studies; or – Studies in the Family of Shakespeareans; or – The Politics of Politics', *Renaissance Quarterly* 4 (4) (Winter 1987).

Bourdieu, Pierre, *Outline of a Theory of Practice*, trans. Richard Nice (Cambridge: Cambridge University Press, 1977).

Boyd, Brian, *On the Origin of Stories: Evolution, Cognition, and Fiction* (Cambridge, MA and London: Harvard University Press, 2009).

Bradshaw, Graham, *Misrepresentations: Shakespeare and the Materialists* (Ithaca, NY: Cornell University Press, 1993).

Braudel, Fernand, *The Mediterranean and the Mediterranean World in the Age of Philip II*, 2 Vols, trans. Siân Reynolds (London: William Collins Sons & Co., 1972–3).

Braudel, Fernand, *Afterthoughts on Material Civilization and Capitalism*, trans. Patricia M. Ranum (Baltimore, MD and London: John Hopkins University Press, 1977).

Braudel, Fernand, *Civilization and Capitalism*, 3 Vols (*The Structures of Everyday Life, The Wheels of Commerce, The Perspective of the World*), trans. Siân Reynolds (New York and London: William Collins Sons & Co., 1981–92).

Bristol, Michael D., *Shakespeare and Moral Agency* (New York and London: Continuum, 2010).

Brooks, Cleanth, *The Well Wrought Urn: Studies in the Structure of Poetry* (New York: Harcourt Brace, 1947).

Bruster, Douglas, *Quoting Shakespeare: Form and Culture in Early Modern Drama* (Lincoln, NE: University of Nebraska Press, 2000).

Bruster, Douglas, *Shakespeare and the Question of Culture: Early Modern Literature and the Cultural Turn* (New York and London: Palgrave Macmillan, 2003).

Burguière, André, *The Annales School: An Intellectual History*, trans. Jane Marie Todd (Ithaca, NY: Cornell University Press, 2009).

Calderwood, James L., *Shakespearean Metadrama* (Minneapolis, MN: University of Minnesota Press, 1971).
Callaghan, Dympna, *Woman and Gender in Renaissance Tragedy: A Study of King Lear, Othello, The Duchess of Malfi and The White Devil* (Hemel Hempstead: Harvester Wheatsheaf, 1989).
Campbell Lily B., *Shakespeare's 'Histories': Mirrors of Elizabethan Policy* (1947; New York and London: Routledge, 2005).
Campbell, Oscar James (ed.), *A Shakespeare Encyclopaedia* (1966; London: Methuen, 1974).
Carroll, Joseph, *Reading Human Nature: Literary Darwinism in Theory and Practice* (Albany, NY: State University Press of New York, 2011)
Chambers, E .K., *William Shakespeare: A Study of Facts and Problems*, 2 Vols (Oxford: Oxford University Press, 1930).
Cohen, Walter, 'Political Criticism of Shakespeare', in *Shakespeare Reproduced: The Text in History and Ideology*, eds Jean E. Howard and Marion F. O'Connor (New York and London: Routledge, 1987).
Coiro, Ann Baynes, and Thomas Fulton, 'Introduction: Old, New, Now', in *Rethinking Historicism from Shakespeare to Milton*, eds Ann Baynes Coiro and Thomas Fulton (Cambridge, Cambridge University Press, 2012), 1–22.
Colebrook, Claire, *New Literary Histories: New Historicism and Contemporary Criticism* (Manchester: Manchester University Press, 1997).
Cook, Amy, *Shakespearean Neuroplay: Reinvigorating the Study of Dramatic Texts and Performance through Cognitive Science* (New York and London: Palgrave Macmillan, 2010).
Crane, Mary Thomas, *Shakespeare's Brain: Reading with Cognitive Theory* (Princeton, NJ: Princeton University Press, 2000).
Cunningham, Valentine, *Reading After Theory* (Malden, MA and Oxford: Blackwell, 2002).
Certeau, Michel, de *The Practice of Everyday Life*, trans. Steven Rendell (Berkeley, CA: University of California Press, 1984).
De Grazia, Margareta and Peter Stallybrass, 'The Materiality of the Shakespearean Text', *Shakespeare Quarterly* 44 (3) (Autumn 1993): 255–83.
De Grazia, Margareta, Maureen Quilligan and Peter Stallybrass, eds, *Subject and Object in Renaissance Culture* (Cambridge: Cambridge University Press, 1996).

DiPietro, Cary and Hugh Grady, eds, *Shakespeare and the Urgency of Now: Criticism and Theory in the 21st Century* (New York and London: Palgrave Macmillan, 2013).

Docherty, Thomas, *After Theory: Postmodernism/Postmarxism* (New York and London: Routledge, 1990).

Dollimore, Jonathan, 'Critical Developments: Cultural Materialism, Feminism and Gender Critique, and New Historicism', in *Shakespeare: A Bibliographical Guide*, ed. Stanley Wells (Oxford: Clarendon Press, 1990).

Dollimore, Jonathan, 'Transgression and Surveillance in *Measure for Measure*', in *Political Shakespeare* eds Jonathan Dollimore and Alan Sinfield, 2nd edn (1985; Manchester: Manchester University Press, 2012).

Dover Wilson, John, *The Fortunes of Falstaff* (1943; Cambridge: Cambridge University Press, 1970).

Dover Wilson, John, *What Happens in Hamlet?*, 3rd edn (1935; Cambridge: Cambridge University Press, 1986).

Dunn, Allen and Thomas F. Haddox, 'The Enigma of Critical Distance; or, Why Historicists Need Convictions', in *The Limits of Literary Historicism*, eds Allen Dunn and Thomas F. Haddox (Knoxville, TN: University of Tennessee Press, 2012).

Eagleton, Terry, *After Theory* (London: Allen Lane, 2003).

Elton, G. R., *The Tudor Revolution in Government: Administrative Changes in the Reign of Henry VIII* (Cambridge: Cambridge University Press, 1953).

Elton, G. R., *Return to Essentials: Some Reflections on the Present State of Historical Study* (1991; Cambridge: Cambridge University Press, 2002).

Elton, G. R., *The Practice of History*, 2nd edn (1967; Oxford: Blackwell, 1992).

Elton, G. R., *England Under the Tudors*, 3rd edn (1955; New York and London: Routledge, 2015).

Empson, William, *Essays on Shakespeare*, ed. David B. Pirie (Cambridge: Cambridge University Press, 1986).

Engels, Friedrich, *The Origin of the Family, Private Property and the State* (1894; New York and London: Penguin, 2010).

Erickson, Peter, 'Review of *Power on Display: The Politics of Shakespeare's Genres* by Leonard Tennenhouse', *Shakespeare Quarterly* 39 (4) (Winter 1988).

Erickson, Peter, *Rewriting Shakespeare, Rewriting Ourselves* (Berkeley, CA: University of California Press, 1991).
Erickson, Peter, 'C. L. Barber', in *Empson, Wilson Knight, Barber, Kott: Great Shakespeareans:, Volume XIII*, ed. Hugh Grady (New York and London: Bloomsbury, 2012).
Erickson, Peter and Coppélia Kahn (eds), *Shakespeare's 'Rough Magic': Renaissance Essays in Honor of C. L. Barber* (Newark, NJ: University of Delaware Press, 1985).
Evans, B. Ifor, *The Language of Shakespeare's Plays* (1952; New York and London: Routledge, 2005).
Felperin, Howard, *The Uses of the Canon: Elizabethan Literature and Contemporary Theory* (Oxford: Clarendon Press, 1990).
Fergusson, Francis, *The Idea of Theater: A Study of Ten Plays, The Art of Drama in Changing Perspective* (1949; Princeton, NJ: Princeton University Press, 1968).
Fergusson, Francis, *Shakespeare: The Pattern in His Carpet* (New York: Delacorte Press, 1970).
Fish, Stanley, 'Commentary: The Young and the Restless', in *The New Historicism*, ed. Harold Aram Veeser (New York and London: Routledge, 1989).
Foucault, Michael, *The Order of Things: Archaeology of the Human Sciences* (1966; London: Routledge, 2002a).
Foucault, Michael, *The Archaeology of Knowledge* (1969; London: Routledge, 2002b).
Foucault, Michael, *Discipline and Punish: The Birth of the Prison*, trans. Alan Sheridan (1977; New York and London: Penguin, 1991).
Foucault, Michael, *The History of Sexuality, Volume 1: The Will to Knowledge*, trans. Robert Hurley (1978; New York and London: Penguin, 1998).
Fraser, Robert, 'Introduction', in James George Frazer, *The Golden Bough: A Study in Magic and Religion*, ed. Robert Fraser (1890–1922; abr. Oxford: Oxford University Press, 1994).
Frazer, James George, *The Golden Bough: A Study in Magic and Religion*, ed. Robert Fraser (1890–1922; abr. Oxford: Oxford University Press, 1994).
Freud, Sigmund, *Totem and Taboo: Resemblances Between the Mental Lives of Savages and Neurotics* (1913; Greentop, MO: Greentop Academic Press, 2011).

Frye, Northrop, *The Anatomy of Criticism: Four Essays* (1957; Princeton, NJ: Princeton University Press, 2000).
Frye, Northrop, *A Natural Perspective: The Development of Shakespearean Comedy and Romance* (New York: University of Columbia Press, 1965).
Fumerton, Patricia, 'Introduction: A New New Historicism', in *Renaissance Culture and the Everyday* (Philadelphia, PA: University of Philadelphia Press, 1999).
Gajowski, Evelyn, 'Beyond Historicism: Presentism, Subjectivity, Politics', *Literature Compass* 7 (8) (2010).
Gallagher, Catherine, and Stephen Greenblatt, *Practising New Historicism* (Chicago, IL and London: University of Chicago Press, 2000).
Garber, Marjorie B., *Shakespeare After All* (New York and London: Random House, 2004).
Gearhart, Suzanne, 'History as Criticism: The Dialogue of History and Literature', *Diacritics* 17 (3) (Autumn 1987).
Geckle, George L., 'Introduction, in *Measure for Measure. Shakespeare: The Critical Tradition*, ed. George L. Geckle (New York and London: The Athlone Press, 2001).
Geertz, Clifford, *The Interpretation of Cultures: Sketched Essays* (New York: Basic Books, 1973).
Giddens, Anthony, *Central Problems in Social Theory: Action, Structure, and Contradiction in Social Analysis* (Berkeley, CA: University of California Press, 1979).
Gless, Darryl J., *Measure for Measure, the Law and the Convent* (Princeton. NJ: Princeton University Press, 1979).
Goldberg, Jonathan, *James I and the Politics of Literature: Jonson, Shakespeare, Donne, and their Contemporaries* (1983; Stanford, CA: Stanford University Press, 1989).
Goldberg, Jonathan, 'Shakespearean Inscriptions: The Voicing of Power', in *Shakespeare's Hand* (Minneapolis, MN: University of Minnesota Press, 2003).
Grady, Hugh, *The Modernist Shakespeare: Critical Texts in a Material World* (Oxford: Clarendon Press, 1991).
Grady, Hugh, *Shakespeare's Universal Wolf: Studies in Early Modern Reification* (Oxford: Clarendon Press, 1996).
Grady, Hugh, 'Theory "After Theory": Christopher Pye's Reading of *Othello*', *Shakespeare Quarterly* 6 (4) (Winter 2009).
Grady, Hugh, (ed.), *Empson, Wilson Knight, Barber, Kott: Great*

Shakespeareans:, Volume XIII, ed. Hugh Grady (New York and London: Bloomsbury, 2012).

Grady, Hugh and Terence Hawkes, 'Introduction: Presenting Presentism', in *Presentist Shakespeares*, eds Hugh Grady and Terence Hawkes (New York and London: Routledge, 2007).

Grav, Peter, 'Taking Stock of Shakespeare and the New Economic Criticism', *Shakespeare* 8 (1) (May 2012): 111–36.

Greenblatt, Stephen, *Renaissance Self-Fashioning: From More to Shakespeare* (1980; Chicago, IL and London: University of Chicago Press, 2005).

Greenblatt, Stephen, 'Introduction', in *The Power of Forms*, ed. Stephen Greenblatt (Norman, OK: Pilgrim Books, 1982).

Greenblatt, Stephen, *Shakespearean Negotiations: The Circulation of Social Energy in Renaissance England* (Berkeley, CA: University of California Press, 1988).

Greenblatt, Stephen, *Learning to Curse: Essays in Early Modern Culture* (1990; New York and London: Routledge, 2007).

Greenblatt, Stephen, (ed.), *New World Encounters* (Berkeley, CA and Oxford: University of California Press, 1993).

Greenblatt, Stephen, *Will in the World: How Shakespeare Became Shakespeare* (New York: W. W. Norton, 2005).

Greenblatt, Stephen, 'Foreword', in *Shakespeare's Festive Comedy: A Study of Dramatic Form and Its Relation to Social Custom*, C. L. Barber, (1959; Princeton, NJ: Princeton University Press, 2012), xi–xvi.

Greenblatt, Stephen, *The Swerve: How the World Became Modern* (New York: W. W. Norton, 2012).

Greene, Gayle, 'The Myth of Neutrality, Again', *Shakespeare Left and Right*, ed. Ivo Kamps (New York and London: Routledge, 1991).

Gutting, Gary, *Michael Foucault's Archaeology of Scientific Reason* (Cambridge: Cambridge University Press, 1989).

Hadfield, Andrew, 'Has Historicism Come Too Far Or, Should We Return to Form?', in *Rethinking Historicism from Shakespeare to Milton*, eds Ann Baynes Coiro and Thomas Fulton (Cambridge, Cambridge University Press, 2012).

Haidt, Jonathan, *The Righteous Mind: Why Good People are Divided by Politics and Religion* (New York and London: Penguin, 2012).

Hapgood, Robert, 'Shakespeare and the Ritualists', *Shakespeare Survey* 15 (1962).

Harpham, Geoffrey Galt, 'Foucault and the New Historicism', *American Literary History* 3 (2) (Summer 1991).

Harris, Jonathan Gil, *Sick Economies: Drama, Mercantilism, and Disease in Shakespeare's England* (University of Pennsylvania Press, 2003).

Harris, Jonathan Gil, *Untimely Matter in the Time of Shakespeare* (Philadelphia, PA: University of Pennsylvania Press, 2008).

Hawkes, David, *Shakespeare and Economic Theory* (New York and London: Bloomsbury Arden, 2015).

Hawkes, Terence, *Meaning By Shakespeare* (New York and London: Routledge, 1992).

Hawkes, Terence, *Shakespeare in the Present* (New York and London: Routledge, 2002).

Hawthorn, Jeremy, *Cunning Passages: New Historicism, Cultural Materialism and Marxism in the Contemporary Literary Debate* (New York and London: Arnold, 1996).

Hays, Michael L., 'Review of *Shakespeare After Theory* by David Scott Kastan', *Comparative Drama* 31 (1) (Spring 2001).

Hidalgo, Pilar, *Paradigms Found: Feminist, Gay and New Historicist Readings of Shakespeare* (Amsterdam: Rodopi, 2001).

Hobbes, Thomas, *Leviathan*, ed. J. C. A. Gaskin (1651; Oxford: Oxford University Press, 2008).

Howard, Jean E., 'Old Wine, New Bottles', *Shakespeare Quarterly* 35 (2) (Summer 1984).

Howard, Jean E., 'The New Historicism in Renaissance Studies', *English Literary Renaissance* 16 (1) (December 1986).

Howard, Jean E., 'Feminism and the Question of History: Resituating the Debate', *Women's Studies: An Interdisciplinary Journal* 19 (2) (1991).

Howard, Jean E. and Marion F. O'Connor, eds, *Shakespeare Reproduced: The Text in History and Ideology* (New York and London: Routledge, 1987).

Howard, Jean E. and Phyllis Rackin, *Engendering a Nation: A Feminist Account of Shakespeare's English Histories* (New York and London: Routledge, 1997).

Hunter, G. K., 'Review of *Shakespeare's Festive Comedy: A Study*

of Dramatic Form and Its Relation to Social Custom by C. L. Barber', *The Review of English Studies* 12 (45) (February 1961).
Hyman, Stanley Edgar, 'The Ritual View of Myth and the Mythic', *The Journal of American Folklore* 68 (270), 'Myth: A Symposium' (October–December 1955).
Hyman, Stanley Edgar, *The Tangled Bank: Darwin, Marx, Frazer and Freud as Imaginative Writers* (New York: Atheneum, 1962).
Jain, Manju, *T. S. Eliot and American Philosophy: The Harvard Years* (Cambridge: Cambridge University Press, 1992).
James I, *The True Law of Free Monarchies; And, Basilikon Doron*, eds Daniel Fisclin and Mark Fortier (Toronto, ON: CRRS Publications, 1996).
Jameson, Fredric, *The Political Unconscious*, 2nd edn (1982; New York and London: Routledge, 2002).
Jameson, Fredric, *Postmodernism, or, The Cultural Logic of Late Capitalism* (Durham, NC: University of Duke Press, 1991).
Jamieson, Michael, 'The Problem Plays, 1920–1970: A Retrospect', *Shakespeare Studies* 25 (1972).
Jardine, Lisa, *Still Harping on Daughters: Women and Drama in the Age of Shakespeare* (Brighton: Harvester Press, 1983).
Johnson, Laurie, John Sutton and Evelyn Tribble, eds, *Embodied Cognition and Shakespeare's Theatre: The Early Modern Body-Mind* (New York and London: Routledge, 2014).
Jones, Ann Rosalind and Peter Stallybrass, *Renaissance Clothing and the Materials of Memory* (Cambridge: Cambridge University Press, 2001).
Jones, Colin and Roy Porter, 'Introduction', in *Reassessing Foucault: Power, Medicine, and The Body* (New York and London: Routledge, 1994).
Jones, Ernest, *Hamlet and Oedipus: A Study into Classic Psychoanalytic Interpretation* (1949; New York: W. W. Norton, 1976).
Kahn, Coppélia, 'The New Historicism And Renaissance Portrayals of Women', *Shakespeare Quarterly* 35 (4) (Winter 1984).
Kamps, Ivo and Karen Ribner, *Measure for Measure: Texts and Contexts* (Boston, MA: St. Martin's, 2004).
Kastan, David Scott, *Shakespeare After Theory* (New York and London: Routledge, 1999).
Kendall, Gillian Murray (ed.), *Shakespearean Power and*

Punishment: A Volume of Essays (Teaneck, NJ: Fairleigh Dickinson University Press, 1998).
Kermode, Frank, *The Patience of Shakespeare* (New York: Harcourt Brace, 1964).
Kermode, Frank, *The Uses of Error* (Cambridge, MA: University of Harvard Press, 1991).
Kermode, Frank, *Shakespeare's Language* (Harmondsworth: Penguin, 2000).
Knight, G. Wilson, *The Wheel of Fire: Interpretations of Shakespearean Tragedy* (1930; New York and London: Routledge, 2002).
Knights, L. C., *Drama and Society in the Age of Jonson* (London: Chatto and Windus, 1937).
Koopman, Colin, *Genealogy as Critique: Foucault and the Problems of Modernity* (Bloomington, IN: University of Indiana Press, 2013).
Korda, Natasha, *Shakespeare's Domestic Economies: Gender and Property in Early Modern England* (Philadelphia, PA: University of Pennsylvania Press, 2002).
LaCapra, Dominick, 'Rethinking Intellectual History and Reading Texts', *History and Theory* 19 (3) (October 1980).
LaCapra, Dominick, *Rethinking Intellectual History: Texts, Contexts, Language* (Ithaca, NY: Cornell University Press, 1983).
LaCapra, Dominick, *History and Criticism* (Ithaca, NY: Cornell University Press, 1985).
Laden, Sonja, 'Recuperating the Archive: Anecdotal Evidence and Questions of "Historical Realism"', *Poetics Today* 25 (1) (Spring 2004).
Lehan, Richard, 'The Theoretical Limits of New Historicism', *New Literary History* 21 (3) (Spring 1990).
Lentricchia, Frank, 'Foucault's Legacy: A New Historicism?', in *The New Historicism*, ed. Harold Aram Veeser (New York and London: Routledge, 1989).
Lenz, Carolyn Ruth Swift, Gayle Greene and Carol Thomas Neely, eds, *The Woman's Part: Feminist Criticism of Shakespeare* (Urbana, IL: University of Illinois Press, 1980).
Lever, J. W., *The Tragedy of State* (London: Methuen, 1971).
Lever, J. W., 'Shakespeare and the Ideas of his Time', *Shakespeare Survey* 29 (1976).

Levin, Richard, *New Readings vs. Old Plays: Recent Trends in the Reinterpretation of Renaissance Drama* (Chicago, IL: University of Chicago Press, 1979).
Levin, Richard, 'Unthinkable Thoughts in the New Historicizing of English Renaissance Drama', *New Literary History* 21 (3) (Spring 1990).
Levin, Richard, 'The Cultural Materialist Attack on Artistic Unity, and the Problem of Ideological Criticism', in *Ideological Approaches to Shakespeare*, eds R. P. Merrix and N. Ranson (Lewiston, NY: Edwin Mellen Press, 1992).
Levin, Richard, '(Re)Thinking Unthinkable Thoughts', *New Literary History* 28 (3) (Summer 1997).
Levin, Richard, 'The Old and the New Materialising of Shakespeare', in *The Shakespearean International Yearbook, Vol. 1: Where Are We Now in Shakespearean Studies?*, eds W. R. Elton and John M. Mucciolo (Brookfield, VT and Aldershot: Ashgate, 1999).
Levin, Richard, *Looking for An Argument: Critical Encounters with the New Approaches to the Criticism of Shakespeare and his Contemporaries* (Madison, NJ: Fairleigh Dickinson University Press, 2003).
Liu, Alan, 'The Power of Formalism: The New Historicism', *English Literary History* 56 (4) (Winter 1989).
Lovejoy, Arthur O., *The Great Chain of Being: A Study of the History of an Idea* (1936; Cambridge, MA: University of Harvard Press, 1976).
Lyne, Raphael, *Shakespeare, Rhetoric, and Cognition* (Cambridge: Cambridge University Press, 2011).
Mahood, M. M., *Shakespeare's Wordplay* (London: Methuen, 1957).
Malinowski, Bronisław, *A Scientific Theory of Culture and Other Essays* (1944; New York and London: Routledge, 2002).
Marcham, Frederick George, 'James I of England and the Little Beagle Letters', in *Persecution and Liberty: Essays in Honor of George Lincoln Burr* (New York: Century Company, 1931).
Marcus, Leah S., *Puzzling Shakespeare: Local Reading and Its Discontents* (Berkeley, CA: University of California Press, 1988).
McCoy, Richard C., 'Lord of Liberty: Francis Davison and the Cult of Elizabeth', in *The Reign of Elizabeth I: Court and Culture*

in the Last Decade, ed. John Guy (Cambridge: Cambridge University Press, 1995).

McLuskie, Kathleen, 'The Patriarchal Bard: Feminist Criticism and Shakespeare: *King Lear* and *Measure for Measure*', in *Political Shakespeare*, eds Jonathan Dollimore and Alan Sinfield, 2nd edn (1985; Manchester: Manchester University Press, 2012).

McMullan, Gordon, 'Preface: Renaissance Configurations', in *Renaissance Configurations: Voices/Bodies/Spaces*, ed. Gordon McMullan (New York and London: Macmillan, 1998).

Miller, James E., Jr., *T. S. Eliot: The Making of an American Poet: 1888–1922* (University Park, PA: University of Pennsylvania Press, 2005).

Montrose, Louis A., 'Renaissance Literary Studies and the Subject of History', *English Literary Renaissance* 16 (1) (December 1986).

Montrose, Louis A., 'Professing the Renaissance: The Poetics and Politics of Culture', in *The New Historicism*, ed. H. Aram Veeser (New York and London: Routledge, 1989).

Montrose, Louis A., 'New Historicisms', in *Redrawing the Boundaries: The Transformation of English and American Literary Studies*, eds Stephen Greenblatt and Giles Gunn (New York: The Modern Language Association of America, 1992).

Montrose, Louis A., *The Purpose of Playing: Shakespeare and the Cultural Politics of the Elizabethan Theater* (Chicago, IL: University of Chicago Press, 1996), 16.

Moulton, Ian Frederick, 'Review', *Shakespeare Quarterly* 6 (3) (Fall 2015).

Mousley, Andy, *Re-Humanising Shakespeare: Literary Humanism, Wisdom and Modernity* (Edinburgh: Edinburgh University Press, 2007).

Mullaney, Steven, *The Place of the Stage: License, Play, and Power in Renaissance England* (1988; Ann Arbor, MI: University of Michigan Press, 2003).

Munslow, Alun, *Deconstructing History*, 2nd edn (1997; New York and London: Routledge, 2006).

Munson, Rebecca and Claude Willan, 'The Children of New Historicism: Literary Scholarship, Professionalization, and the Will to Publish', in *The Limits of Literary Historicis*, eds Allen Dunn and Thomas F. Haddox (Knoxville, TN: University of Tennessee Press, 2012).

Neely, Carol Thomas, 'Constructing the Subject: Feminist Practice and the New Renaissance Discourses', *English Literary Renaissance* (December 1988).
Newman, Karen, *Fashioning Femininity and English Renaissance Drama* (Chicago, IL: University of Chicago Press, 1991).
Nuttall, A. D., *A New Mimeses: Shakespeare and the Representation of Reality*, 2nd edn (1983; New Haven, CT: Yale University Press, 2007a).
Nuttall, A. D., *Shakespeare: The Thinker* (New Haven, CT: Yale University Press, 2007b).
Orgel, Stephen, *The Illusion of Power: Political Theater in the English Renaissance* (Berkeley, CA: University of California Press, 1975).
Orgel, Stephen and Roy C. Strong, *Inigo Jones: Theatre of the Stuart Court*, 2 Vols (London: Sotheby Parke Bernet, 1973).
Orr, Linda, 'The Revenge of Literature: A History of History', *New Literary History* 18 (1) (Autumn 1986).
Papadopoulou, Theodora, 'Circulating through "Languages and Tales": Stephen Greenblatt's *Cardenio*', in *Reinventing the Renaissance*, eds Sarah Annes Brown, Robert I. Lublin and Lynsey McCulloch (New York and London: Palgrave Macmillan, 2013).
Parvini, Neema, *Shakespeare's History Plays: Rethinking Historicism* (Edinburgh: Edinburgh University Press, 2012a).
Parvini, Neema, *Shakespeare and Contemporary Theory: New Historicism and Cultural Materialism* (New York and London: Bloomsbury, 2012b).
Parvini, Neema, 'The Scholars and The Critics: Shakespeare studies and theory in the 2010s', *Shakespeare* 10 (2) (Spring 2014).
Parvini, Neema, *Shakespeare and Cognition: Thinking Fast and Slow Through Character* (New York and London: Palgrave Macmillan, 2015).
Parvini, Neema, 'Cultural Materialism', in *The Edinburgh Companion to Critical Theory*, ed. Stuart Sim (Edinburgh: Edinburgh University Press, 2016).
Pechter, Edward, 'The New Historicism and Its Discontents: Politicizing Renaissance Drama', *PMLA* 102 (3) (May 1987).
Pechter, Edward, 'Making Love to Our Employment; Or, the Immateriality of Arguments about the Materiality of the Shakespearean Text', *Textual Practice* 11 (1) (1997).

Pieters, Jürgen, *Moments of Negotiation: The New Historicism of Stephen Greenblatt* (Amsterdam: Amsterdam University Press, 2001).
Pinker, Stephen, *The Blank Slate: The Modern Denial of Human Nature* (New York and London: Penguin, 2002).
Quarmby, Kevin A., 'Narrative of Negativity: Whig Historiography and the Spectre of King James in *Measure for Measure*', in *Shakespeare Survey 64: Shakespeare as Cultural Catalyst*, ed. Peter Holland (Cambridge: Cambridge University Press, 2011).
Rabkin, Norman, *Shakespeare and the Common Understanding* (New York: The Free Press, 1967).
Rackin, Phyllis, *Stages of History: Shakespeare's English Chronicles* (Ithaca, NY: Cornell University Press, 1990).
Reese M. M.; *The Cease of Majesty: A Study of Shakespeare's History Plays* (New York: St. Martin's Press, 1961).
Robson, Mark, *Stephen Greenblatt* (New York and London: Routledge, 2007).
Rossiter, A. P., *Angel with Horns: Fifteen Lectures on* Shakespeare (1961; New York and Harlow: Longman, 1989).
Sahlins, Marshall, *Islands of History* (Chicago, IL: University of Chicago Press, 1985).
Sajdek, Bruce T., *Shakespeare Index: An Annotated Bibliography of Critical Articles on the Plays 1959–1983*, 2 Vols (Millwood, NY: Kraus International Publications, 1992).
Sanders, Wilbur, *The Dramatist and the Received Idea: Studies in the Plays of Marlowe and Shakespeare* (Cambridge: Cambridge University Press, 1968).
Sartre, Jean-Paul, *What Is Literature?*, trans. Bernard Fretchman (New York: Philosophical Library, 1947).
Segal, Robert A., *The Myth and Ritual Theory: An Anthology* (Oxford: Blackwell, 1998).
Shuger, Deborah, 'The "I" of the Beholder: Renaissance Mirrors and the Reflexive Mind', in *Renaissance Culture and the Everyday* (Philadelphia, PA: University of Philadelphia Press, 1999).
Simpson, David, 'Touches of the Real', *London Review of Books* 23 (10) (May 2001).
Skura, Meredith Anne, 'Discourse and the Individual: The Case of Colonialism in *The Tempest*', *Shakespeare Quarterly* 40 (1) (Spring 1989).

Smith, Peter J., 'The Critical Backstory', in *Richard III: A Critical Reader*, ed. Annaliese Connolly (New York and London: Bloomsbury Arden, 2013).

Spurgeon, Caroline, *Shakespeare's Imagery and What It Tells Us* (1935; Cambridge: Cambridge University Press, 1979).

Stanislawski, Dan, 'Review of *The Mediterranean and the Mediterranean World in the Age of Philip II* by Fernand Braudel', American Geographical Society 64 (4) (October 1974).

Stevenson, David, '"The Gudeman of Ballangeich": Rambles in the Afterlife of James V', *Folklore* 115 (2) (August 2004): 187–200.

Stone, Lawrence, 'History and Post-Modernism', *Past & Present* 131 (May 1991).

Taylor, Michael, *Shakespeare: Criticism in the Twentieth Century* (Oxford: Oxford University Press, 2001).

Tennenhouse, Leonard, *Power on Display: The Politics of Shakespeare's Genres* (1986; New York and London: Routledge, 2010).

Thomas, Brook, *The New Historicism and Other Old-Fashioned Topics* (Princeton, NJ: Princeton University Press, 1991).

Tillyard, E. M. W., *The Elizabethan World Picture* (1942; London: Vintage, 1959).

Tillyard, E. M. W., *Shakespeare's History Plays* (1944; New York and London: Penguin, 1991).

Tribble, Evelyn, *Cognition in the Globe: Attention and Memory in Shakespeare's Theatre* (New York and London: Palgrave Macmillan, 2011).

Tricomi, Albert H., *Reading Tudor-Stuart Texts through Cultural Historicism* (Gainesville, FL: University Press of Florida, 1996).

Vann, Richard T., 'The Reception of Hayden White', *History and Theory* 37 (2) (May 1998).

Veeser, Harold Aram, 'Introduction', in *The New Historicism*, ed. Harold Aram Veeser (New York and London: Routledge, 1989).

Veeser, Harold Aram, 'The New Historicism', in *The New Historicism Reader*, ed. Harold Aram Veeser (New York and London: Routledge, 1994a).

Veeser, Harold Aram, 'Review of *The New Historicism and Other Old-Fashioned Topics* by Brook Thomas', *Modern Philology* 91 (3) (February 1994b).

Vickers, Brian, *Appropriating Shakespeare: Contemporary Critical Quarrels* (New Haven, CT: Yale University Press, 1993).

Vickers, Brian, 'General Editor's Preface', in *Measure for Measure. Shakespeare: The Critical Tradition* ed. George L. Geckle (New York and London: The Athlone Press, 2001).
Wallace, David Foster, 'Authority and American Usage', in *Consider the Lobster and Other Essays* (New York: Little Brown and Co., 2005), 66–127.
Watts, Cedric, *William Shakespeare: Measure for Measure* (New York and London: Penguin, 1986).
Waugh, Patricia, *Literary Theory and Criticism: An Oxford Guide* (Oxford: Oxford University Press, 2006).
Wayne, Valerie (ed.), *The Matter of Difference: Materialist Feminist Criticism of Shakespeare* (Hemel Hempstead: Harvester Wheatsheaf, 1991a).
Wayne, Valerie (ed.), 'Introduction', in *The Matter of Difference: Materialist Feminist Criticism of Shakespeare*, ed. Valerie Wayne (Hemel Hempstead: Harvester Wheatsheaf, 1991b).
Weimann, Robert, *Shakespeare and the Popular Tradition in the Theatre: Studies in the Social Dimension of Dramatic Form and Function*, ed. Robert Schwartz (1978; Baltimore, MD: John Hopkins University Press, 1987).
Weisinger, Herbert 'The Myth and Ritual Approach to Shakespearean Tragedy' (1964), in *The Myth and Ritual Theory: An Anthology*, ed. Robert A. Segal (Oxford: Blackwell, 1998).
Wells, Robin Headlam, 'The Fortunes of Tillyard', *English Studies* 65 (5) (1985).
Wells, Robin Headlam, 'Historicism and "Presentism" in Early Modern Studies', *The Cambridge Quarterly* 29 (1) (2000).
Wells, Robin Headlam, *Shakespeare's Humanism* (Cambridge: Cambridge University Press, 2005).
Wells, Robin Headlam, *Shakespeare's Politics: A Contextual Introduction* (New York and London: Continuum, 2009).
Westermarck, Edward, *The History of Human Marriage*, 3 Vols (London: Macmillan, 1891).
Westermarck, Edward, *The Origin and Development of Moral Ideas*, 2 Vols (London: Macmillan, 1906).
Wharton, T. F., *Measure for Measure: The Critics Debate* (London: Macmillan, 1989).
White, Hayden, 'The Burden of History', *History and Theory* 5 (2) (1966).

Williams, Raymond, *Marxism and Literature* (Oxford: Oxford University Press, 1977).
Wilson, Richard, 'Introduction: Historicising New Historicism', in *New Historicism and Renaissance Drama*, eds Richard Wilson and Richard Dutton (New York and London: Longman, 1992), 1.
Wilson, Scott, *Cultural Materialism: Theory and Practice* (Oxford: Blackwell, 1995).
Woodbridge, Linda, *Women and the English Renaissance: Literature and the Nature of Womankind, 1540 to 1620* (Urbana, IL: University of Illinois Press, 1984).
Worden, Blair, 'Tolerant Repression', *London Review of Books* 12 (9) (May 1990).
Yachnin, Paul and Jessica Slights, eds, *Shakespeare and Character: Theory, History, Performance, and Theatrical Persons* (New York and London: Palgrave Macmillan, 2009).

INDEX

Pages in bold denote principal subject areas that are discussed in depth.